# Transmutare

## Shelia Bolt Rudesill

# DEDICATION

To everyone who has been loved in spite of themselves

# ACKNOWLEDGEMENTS

To Bud Rudesill for support, encouragement, praise, proofreading, editing, formatting, and especially believing that a nurse without writing credentials can be an author too.

To Lanna Richards for always holding my hand over the phone and internet and boosting my confidence. This book may not have been published without her years of inspiration.

To Sheila Willensky, Assistant Editor, *Arizona Jewish Press*, for assistance with and editing Jewish Content

To my friend Alvin Schultzberg for mentoring Jewish content

To my friends and colleagues at Pittsboro Writers Morning Out, sponsored by The NC Writers' Network

To a wonderful group of proofreaders who know how to critique honestly: Sharon Graham, Bonnie Olsen, and Martha Bolt

To The New Orleans Chamber of Commerce

Websites: Judaism 101, Ritual Well, My Jewish Learning

Blog: Jewish in a Gentile World

Books: *Beginning Anew, a Woman's Companion to the High Holy Days*, Gail Twersky Reimer and Judith A. Kates and *The Creative Jewish Wedding Book*, Gabrielle Kaplan-Mayer

And to all those who love my stories, some of whom I've yet to meet, my heartfelt gratitude.

## 1

Ben Lowenstein flew. We were eight-enchanting-years-old and he had a crush on me that made butterflies tickle my insides. The moment his feet left the highest diving board of the city pool, I began to clap. Ben's smile was one of proud accomplishment—he was showing off for my benefit and he knew that I knew. Before he crashed through the surface of the chlorinated water, his legs and arms splayed as if he were backtracking or had changed his mind. The thud of Ben's head against the bottom of the pool sliced through my side allowing the butterflies to pour from me before a permanent aching set in. Ben Lowenstein had broken his neck. A numbing stillness diffused through me like ether, as if in that moment of terror I'd been put to sleep to dream only of the beautiful bronze-skinned boy sailing against the backdrop of an azure sky.

For the next few weeks Ben was the topic of conversation. All I could envision was a marionette, its parts in a jumbled mass on the stage floor. However, Ben neither got up nor walked away like Pinocchio did. He never walked again, even with strings and wire and operations. Just like the plucking of a flower from a vine, his head became a separate entity from his body—an animated brain unable to communicate with its inert components.

"Ms. Segal, could you repeat that?" My neurology professor brings me back to the present.

Embarrassed by my nightmarish frown, I raise my hand to cover my mouth and fake a cough. "Excuse me. Yes, sir. My goal is spinal cord rejuvenation."

"Don't you mean rehabilitation?"

"No, sir. I mean to put severed spinal cords back together…so the patient can regain total control. I want to completely obliterate paralysis."

"I think you might consider transferring to seminary, Ms. Segal." The professor leans into the mike. His reproachful words vibrate. "You don't want to be a doctor, you want to be God."

His smirk turns my stomach contents to week-old buttermilk. Giggles and whispers echo in my ears and I wonder what kind of doctors the other students intend to be.

"If there was a god out there, we wouldn't need doctors." I shout above the commotion.

He glares over the top of his half-moon spectacles. "Class dismissed."

How humiliating. I slink from the noisy classroom feeling the buttermilk churn. God? Is that who I sound like? A god who picks up innocent children in a vortex of cruelty only to spit them out shattered beyond repair? No, I don't want to be God. I just want to find the tiny link that will reunite nerve cells. How impossible can that be?

When I turn on my phone there are six messages—two from Katie, three from Beka, one from Mama. I dial Beka first.

Both Katie and I are planning our weddings and our marvelous friend Beka, an aspiring haute couture fashion designer, is on her way from Manhattan with design ideas for our entire wedding collections. Tonight will be the celebration of her gifts to us. When she picks up I speak before she has the chance. "Where are you?" I can only imagine Beka's excitement—sitting behind the wheel, radio blaring, sunroof open, while her auburn hair billows in the wind. At least I think it's still auburn. For the past few years she's experimented with hair color, even had a hot pink streak down one side for a while. She often threatens to cut it short enough for gelled spikes. She may do it someday but I doubt she'll ever have the nerve to part with those silky tresses that swing when she moves like a L'Oreal Paris model. Beka is smaller boned and shorter than me, cuter too especially since she got a nose job a few years back. Even though we talk on the phone several times a day, I can't wait to see her in person.

"I'm in southern Virginia, just about to North Carolina," she says. "I'm so excited about showing off my designs. How is your day going?"

"Great, now that I'm out of class. The prof accused me of wanting to be God."

"Oy gevalt. You told him about Ben, didn't you?"

"No, but I was thinking about the day he broke his neck. I just stated my goal. I want to put spinal cords back together. What's so pompous about that?"

"He sounds like one of those PhDs who only believe in their own opinion. You know how full of themselves academicians are."

"Thanks for reminding me."

"Hey, I just passed the North Carolina state line."

"So, you should hit Katie's about the same time I do." I reach my car, throw my backpack into the rear seat. "I have to stop at the library on my way."

"Good. I love you. I can't wait to show you my designs. You're going to love them, dahling. I just know it."

As I pull out of the med school parking lot, I dial Katie's cell but her voice mail picks up, so I dial her work number.

"Collins, Collins, and Rice, this is Katherine McFarling. How may I help you?"

"I just adore your professional side."

"Shelli, I'm so nervous." Katie speaks in a hushed voice. I can tell she's trembling.

"You're working late."

"Yeah. Just finished up an involved deposition for Matt Collins. He needed it the day before yesterday. You know how it goes. I just tracked down the plaintiff a couple hours ago. I'm finished now. I'm actually gathering my stuff to get out of here."

"Yeah, I'm hightailing it too."

"Why? What happened?" Katie sounds like a typical Jewish mother, except that she's an Irish Catholic.

"Nothing, really. I was just the butt of a joke in class. I'll tell you all about it later. Why are you nervous?"

"Promise you won't say anything to Beka?"

"Promise."

"Well, what if we don't like our gowns? You know, just what if we don't? Or what if I like yours better than mine or you like mine better than yours? We can't hurt Beka's feelings. We just can't."

I bite the fat of my thumb, try not to laugh. Beka knows us better than we know ourselves, especially when it comes to fashion and personalities. She's helped us shop for clothes and always picked the perfect outfit, even if we didn't agree at the moment. Katie seems to have forgotten this.

"Our wedding gowns have to be simply perfect." Katie sounds panicked now. "I mean we *have* to like them. What if we don't? What will it do to Beka?"

"We won't hurt her feelings. The gowns will be perfect. Just trust her." There's a long silence on Katie's end. "Are you there? Katie?"

"I'm here. I know you're right. It's just that—"

"Stop a minute. Focus on how absolutely perfect everything is going to be. You'll see."

Katie sighs one of her long worrisome sighs. "I'll feel better when you get here."

After my pit stop at the library, I head down Hwy 55 from Duke University. I dodge a deer then a troupe of reckless Friday-after-work drivers. I squirm in my seat. Imagine my prof suggesting I transfer to seminary.

I stop at a red light, close my eyes, and breathe deeply until the car behind me and the one behind him honk their horns. I open my eyes again and punch the accelerator. My goals are *not* lofty. Who is he to put me down?

This morning's conversation with Mama floats across my mind. I should call her, but I don't. In recent years we've grown apart, something I never thought could be. Most of it stems from religion. When I left for college, I left my Jewish orthodox upbringing behind. I can't buy into a god who allows people to suffer. My whole family thinks God will sustain them in the face of despair. When all hope is lost, He'll guide them toward the sunrise that will suddenly pierce their darkness and bless their souls with the glorious light of day. Ha. These poetic words fail to address the fact that this is not my reality. I breathe a sigh of relief. There is no darkness around me. Why can't Mama see that? My life is filled with glorious, brilliant, magnificent light.

I drive past several strip malls that just a few years ago were tobacco farms and cow pastures. Turning off the highway, I follow a two-lane road lined with Victorian houses in every condition from immaculately renovated with wrought iron fences to dilapidated hovels complete with Confederate flags, lawns turned to weeds, and Harley-Davidsons in the driveways. Katie's townhouse is here in Apex, a charming southern town struggling to survive the urban sprawl of the Triangle—Raleigh, Durham, and Chapel Hill.

We greet with our usual kiss on the cheek. Katie invites me to sit at the dining room table. She plops down across from me tapping her magenta fingernails on the shiny veneer surface. She suddenly looks up as if she'd forgotten I was here. "I have a bottle of champagne…to celebrate everything." My fair friend brushes away ginger curls that hang too long over her eyebrows. "I just can't wait for Beka to get here so we can open it."

"Are you still nervous?" I grin at her, as she walks to the fridge, her tight ringlets bounce halfway down her back. She pulls a bottle of Gloria Ferrer from the bottom shelf.

"No, well, maybe yes." She returns to the table and struggles to remove the cork from the bottle. After several unsuccessful attempts, she lets out a long defeated sigh.

I reach for the bottle. "Give it 'ere, me darlin' Kate," I say in as much an Irish brogue as a Jewish girl can muster then open the bottle with two twists letting just a hint of a hiss escape.

Katie produces three flutes, each with a different color stem and each decorated with curling ribbons in bright jewel colors. She's been to Pier 1, I think, as the smile inside me rolls and fizzes faster than the bubbles of champagne race to the top of the flute. I pretend not to know what she's up to. She fills the flutes to the top then lifts hers to click with mine in a silent toast. I smile into her ocean-green eyes and see a lingering hint of nervousness.

Katie slowly sets her glass on the table. "It's just that—"

"We've been through it already. We'll love the gowns, believe me, we will. Beka is so proud of what she's designed."

"Here's to Beka." Katie raises her glass again but doesn't put it to her lips. "Oh my God. I almost forgot." She whips around, picks up a red plastic shopping bag, pulls out a can of Silly String, and sprays me before I can duck. "Here," she says, laughing now. She reaches into the bag to pull out a hot pink, fake boa, and a plastic silver tiara. "Catch." She throws both my way.

"Yuck." I try to remove as much of the Silly String as I can then place the tiara on my head and wrap the boa around my neck before grabbing the bag away from her. I dump the contents on the table. "What's this?" I feign innocence, looking at the assortment of gaily cellophane-wrapped dried fruits, beribboned chocolate candies, and tiny boxes of assorted pastries.

Katie laughs while she pulls her turtleneck sweater off over her head revealing a sexy black satin camisole with a matching bow tie. She reaches into a second bag for a silver top hat with glitter and a cigarette holder with a fake cigarette that produces smoke as she blows into it.

"Leave it to you to remember what day it is." I reach for a box of raspberry-filled triangular pastries. "This isn't exactly a major holy day."

"I know but it's my favorite. Today we celebrate the day Queen Esther saved the Jews from the Persians." Katie tips her hat. Her voice sounds more like a kindergarten teacher than a Playboy bunny. "A day for feasting, laughter, and carousing. Now drink up. You're supposed to drink wine and make merry today."

"You maven," I say as we raise our glasses once again.

"Cheers." Katie holds her glass high.

"Today it's L'chaim. It's Purim, remember?"

"Oh, sorry. You're right. "L'chaim." She hugs my neck. "Just takes one sip of wine to forget what we're celebrating."

"You'd better pour a little in that third glass. A car just pulled up outside."

"Beka, Beka, Beka. Just wait till you see what I have for you," Katie speaks in as lurid a voice as one so innocent can conjure up. Rummaging through the costume bag, she pulls out just what she wants for Beka—a black lace bustier and a blond Lady Gaga wig.

I can't help but laugh watching Katie rush to the door with her holiday regalia and a can of Silly String. Beka will be surprised but not shocked. Being Jewish by birth doesn't mean she'll remember Purim—Judaism's most dramatic and fun-filled holiday. She's not that into Judaism.

Before Beka can ring the bell, Katie swings the door open but seeing her loaded down with boxes, a briefcase, and her laptop, Katie refrains from spraying. "Beka, It's so good to see you. Isn't this just the most exciting day of our lives?"

Beka places her gear on the floor while Katie puts the wig haphazard on her head before she douses her with Silly String.

Beka brushes the Silly String away before throwing me a kiss. "Oy vay, is it Halloween already?"

I hand Beka a glass of champagne before pulling her into a hug. "Drink up. Indulge her, Bek." I raise my eyebrows. "She's the only Christian on earth who celebrates Purim."

"How could I forget?" Beka guzzles the champagne like a cowboy throws down a shot of whiskey. She lets out a magnificent belch. "Excuse me," she says, spluttering then holds out the glass for more. "We should drink until we don't know good from evil. That's the tradition, isn't it?"

"One of them." Katie pours more champagne and Beka sips it this time.

"But aren't our costumes supposed to be Persian? I mean shouldn't I be dressed up like Esther instead of Gaga?" Beka chides with her sarcastic grin.

"Supposed to be but I'm sure Queen Esther wouldn't mind how we celebrate. She just wants us to celebrate." Katie grins in triumph.

"Oy, Save me from this shiksa, will you, Shelli?"

"Come on, Beka, get your bustier on, and come sit between us for a selfie. We have to have a picture together on this incredible day."

We exchange a wink and Beka does as directed.

"Wait," Katie says. Where's my cigarette holder? Oh, there it is on the bar."

I click off several shots and we're captured together in a state of bliss for the thousandth time, at least.

The flash stings my eyes and when I close them I see the three of us sitting on the sides of a sandbox on the day we became this wonderful threesome.

~*~

Our first day of kindergarten was unusually hot and humid. The sun streaked through the heavy morning mist turning the usually invisible no-see-ums bright white. Dust particles reflected the light and hung suspended like stars in the silvery stillness. At the far end of the playground, Beka and I spotted her—a frail, red-haired girl sitting on the side of the sandbox, feet completely submerged in the white sand as if she were trying to sink into oblivion.

"What's wrong with her?" I asked, expecting Beka to know.

She shrugged. "Let's go see."

We sat, one of us on each side of her, watching her chest heave as she stopped her crying to look at us for a long moment before she told us her horror. An argument between her parents the night before had left blood running down her mother's face and the sound of screeching tires as her father sped away from the flashing blue lights of a police car that stood with doors wide open in the middle of the front lawn.

I remember recoiling, grabbing at the neck of my Hello Kitty T-shirt. An argument was more than I could imagine, especially one that ended in blood and police in the front yard. I thought of the way my parents smiled when they discussed issues, like when Beka and I insisted they let us attend a secular kindergarten with mostly Southern Baptist kids.

For once in her life Beka sat silent, wiping her nose on her sleeve, swallowing tears.

We sat quietly, each in our own little world of oppressive horror, denial, and disbelief. "What's your name?" I asked when words stopped evading me.

"Katie."

"I'm Shelli," I said. "This is Beka."

Katie reached out, squeezed our hands. I'd seen adults shake hands or embrace but I'd never greeted another child with such formality. The gesture wasn't entirely formal. It was more a plea for comfort, for friendship.

That was the first time Beka and I had let anyone in. We'd been best friends since before we could remember. Born two months apart, Mama figures we bonded the day we met. We shared a crib the first Saturday of my life in Beth Israel's nursery and we sucked slobber off each other's fists. My mother was so touched by this she vowed we'd be friends for life no matter that Beka's mother was a mere acquaintance. When the Schultzbergs turned from organized religion, Mama devised ways to keep Beka and me together—public kindergarten being one of them. The Schultzbergs couldn't afford a Jewish private school like my doctor-father could so Beka and I finally got to go to school with the Baptists.

Until we were five, Beka and I looked like twins but the next year I had a growth spurt and towered inches above her. We were brawny and vivacious to the point of being cheeky. We took risks like sliding down the slide at the neighborhood pool in tandem or head first on our backs, ignoring the lifeguard's whistle. We painted eyeliner on each other with finger paints while the teacher wasn't looking. More than once we were separated into time-out where we knew better than to look at each other for fear we'd burst out laughing. Katie softened our edges while we brushed layers of shyness from her.

We cried so much that first day of kindergarten that the other kids branded us "the slobber sisters." Even then I knew that nothing, come hell or high water, would ever separate us.

~*~

Beka gets up from the table, stoops to take a file folder from one of the boxes. "These are for your attendants, if you like them," she says. She sounds a little hesitant. Uh oh, I think, Katie isn't the only one whose nerves are on edge.

I take the folder. Before I open it I notice Katie's quivering lip. She looks as if she might burst out crying. I look away to gaze at Beka's sketches inside. "Beka. These are incredible." I remove the tiara and boa then pull my thick, dark hair away from my face, tying it in two knots behind my head.

Beka smiles. Katie blows air through pursed lips.

"This is exactly what I dreamed of—simple, casual, elegant." The designs are sleek—corset tops with modestly flowing floor-length A-line skirts. I lean to give Beka a hug. Not just for the brilliant designs, but to ease her nerves. "They're more than marvelous." I let my hand rest on the page. Until now, the wedding seemed distant but seeing the sketches of the gowns makes my dreams come alive. It's really happening. My perfect life will soon hold memories of a perfect wedding to a perfect man. "I love you, Beka. How can I ever thank you for this?" I wipe the tears that flow freely down my cheeks.

"I don't need thanks. I'm doing this because I want to. This is my gift to you because I love you too. Now, stop blubbering or you'll have us all in tears."

With one hurdle over, Beka seems less nervous, more herself—Ms. Independent. Going back to one of the boxes, she pulls out swatches of fabric wrapped in tissue. "For the dresses to hang properly, I chose this heavier silk. I'm pretty sure I've chosen the right colors."

As Beka opens the tissue paper, the glorious colors of zinnias fly out to thrill my senses. I wipe away more tears with the back of my hand before I touch the fabric. "What kind of silk is this? I love the texture. Look how it catches the light in places and casts shadows in others."

"Douppioni silk." Beka lets out a little chuckle. "It's a silk that's produced from two silkworms that spin a cocoon together. They produce a double thread. I thought it would be romantic for a wedding."

Katie puckers her lips, sends me an air kiss.

All I can do is smile. The vibrant colors match my excitement. At once I choose a color for each attendant. Hot pink for Saphira, my sister. Purple for Rachel, my sister-in-law. Gold for my seven-year-old niece, Anna. Deep rose for my youngest niece, Naomi. Yes, deep rose will brighten Naomi's pale skin.

It's difficult to imagine what Naomi looks like now. She has a tiny tumor on her brain and lost her hearing in one ear. I shake the image of her that my brother has painted of pallor, lethargy, and weight loss. I remember her the way I last saw her—a giggling, robust little girl who'd just lost her first tooth. We've always had a special connection, something so unlike my relationships with her sister and my two nephews. It's like our hearts are in sync. We're magnetized to each other. It seems that we knew each other before we were born.

I push Naomi to the recesses of my mind, take a big breath then return to my wedding plans. "Beka, you're going to wear yellow." I smile and she smiles back. "Katie, I want you to wear the watermelon. My two favorite colors for my two best friends."

"Won't watermelon clash with my hair?"

"Watermelon will bring out the highlights in your red hair. See?" I hold the watermelon swatch close to Katie's face. "You'll be gorgeous. Besides, you don't particularly like yellow but it's Beka's favorite. She looks great in it too. I can't wait to see us all dressed up." I can barely contain my happiness. "Now, I'm dying to see what you've come up with for me."

Beka smiles. "I'm saving your gowns for last." Beka turns to Katie. "I had a little difficulty with your bridesmaid's gowns, Katie. Hopefully, I haven't gone overboard."

A look of near hysteria covers Katie's face. "Overboard?"

"Like green. How boring. An Irish green Catholic wedding is almost beyond my scope."

Katie huffs, folds her arms across her chest. Beka is teasing her but she doesn't get it. "My wedding is going to be teal green, not Irish green."

Beka takes in a long breath while she slowly pulls out another file. "I went way out on a limb, Katie. I'm almost afraid to show this to you. In fact…" She opens her laptop, punches at the keys. "The gown looks better on screen. "The idea excited me so much that I had to make a prototype."

"Really? A prototype?" Katie looks as if she'll faint from either elation or trepidation. She kneels next to Beka, face level with the computer screen. Seeing Beka dressed in the gown, she gasps. "I love it. It's not like anything I'd have picked out or even imagined but oh, it's so classy."

"Let me see." I move behind Katie for a better view. "Your internship with Vera Wang is showing. Stunning. The color isn't Irish green at all. What color is it?"

"Green topaz, it's not really teal, it's more the color of the ocean at mid-day. It's one of the new colors for the fall collections." Beka reaches into her briefcase and pulls out a swatch of fabric.

"Why, it's almost the exact color of our Katie's eyes." I rest one hand on Katie's shoulder, the other on Beka's.

"Look at the way the gown hugs the body and then poufs out one side. So different from the ubiquitous mermaid." Katie studies the design, her eyes bright. "It gives the illusion of a train, doesn't it?"

"It's windswept and elegant," I say. "Very elegant."

Katie shakes tears away. "You're gifted, Beka. Really, you are."

"That's just the reaction I'd hoped for. I knew you wanted formal but was afraid this would be too much. I didn't spend almost six years and fifty million dollars on college and grad school for nothing." Beka sits back, sips her champagne like she would after a long day's work is done.

"I wish you were getting married too." Katie says with a look of longing.

"Marriage. Not so certain it's for me."

"What?" I say.

"With all this excitement, I can't stop thinking about the day my family fell apart. We were twelve then." Beka nips on her pinky. Her eyes stare into a vastness.

"Your family didn't fall apart." I bite my bottom lip. "Your father did."

"That's right." Katie glances down to her twisting hands. "It's up to us to do better than our parents."

I shift in my chair, hold out my glass. "I'm ready for a refill. Let's drink to happiness."

"Let's drink to happy marriages." Katie empties the bottle into our glasses.

Beka shakes her head. "You should never know from human misery. You should only know happiness—that's what my mother kept telling me when Dad left, especially when I finally realized that he'd never return. Maybe I'm trying to avoid that kind of human misery."

## 2

"Quick, someone remind me. Why do I want to get married?" Katie shrieks, pulling at her shiny curls.

"Because you and Sean have already made the commitment to love each other. You just said that you wouldn't make the same mistakes your parents did."

Katie lets go of her hair. "How can you be so sure?"

"Because I believe in you to make it right. Your relationship with Sean was meant to be. That's all there is to it."

"Shut up." Katie smiles shyly as rivulets of crimson grow up her neck like a perfusion of rose petals until her face is just a shade or two lighter than her hair. She's always been the one most easily embarrassed. She cries over everything—dying things, kittens chasing butterflies, even schmaltzy TV commercials. Some think she's sentimental but she's not clueless. With such unassuming grace, she worked her way through Loyola with part-time jobs, student loans, and grants, hell-bent to become a ruthless paralegal with a prestigious law firm.

"It's true." I reiterate. "You and Sean were meant to be when you bought that ticket to the Saints' game. Who would've thought that Sean, a good Catholic boy, would have a seat right next to yours? The two of you are going to make beautiful babies who love football."

"Enough schmoozing already." Beka picks up a second folder. "Anyone interested in wedding gowns?"

"Of course we are." Katie begins to pace. "I just can't imagine that my gown can be more stunning than the bridesmaid's."

"Well, it is. I wanted something elegant, yet delicate like you but not too froufrou or Shirley Temple if you know what I mean."

"Like sexy, in a sweet way?" I wink at Beka. We both know that Katie isn't a Barbie kind of bride. In my dreams, that's what I want to be.

"This gown isn't sexy at all...it's provocative. In fact, I was so certain that this is the dress for you that it's already made." Beka is solemn, anxious. "It's in the car, ready for a fitting."

I feel a surge of excitement but Katie stands transfixed, looking as if she'll faint. "Tonight, Katie," I say. "A fitting right now."

"Are you alright, Katie?" Beka takes hold of her arm to steady her.

Katie tilts her head in a quick, small nod. "I just didn't expect to see the...the finished dress."

"When I thought about your wedding, I thought about the setting. The New Orleans part was simple but the Saint Louis Cathedral threw me for a loop. That place was built in the eighteenth century and is filled with history. Did you know that the Louisiana Purchase was signed there? The building has survived major environmental catastrophes, yet it still stands strong—the way you want your marriage to be." Beka raises her eyebrows. "Your gown had to match, had to be formal, yet fit into not only southern Louisiana elegance but the French architectural essence created by the Baroness Pontalba—who is responsible for adding a bit of Paris to the cathedral as well as the New Orleans landscape. I knew I had my work cut out for me. When I finally visualized the gown, I couldn't stop thinking about it until it was finished."

"I've never seen you so excited, Beka." I feel the anticipation build for the unveiling of this creation.

"Just let me get the dress. I'll meet you in your bedroom." Beka almost floats to the door, her feet barely touch the ground. She's pleased with herself, I can tell, and not nervous now but self-assured, excited to show us another masterpiece.

"Come on, Katie, let's get you ready for this." When we reach the top of the stairs I notice an other-worldly expression on Katie's face. "It's going to be grand. You're going to love it. Just keep breathing."

Everything is impeccably in place in Katie's bedroom, just like the rest of her house, like those too flawless rooms in a *Southern Living* magazine. She looks at her reflection in the mirror, removes the top hat, fluffs out her hair.

During visits with her father—who'd picked up and moved to Louisiana as soon as his divorce was final—Katie fell in love with New Orleans. When she first stepped inside St. Louis Cathedral with its wide, sinking black and white tile floor reflecting filtered light from large stained-glass windows, she had a vision of her wedding taking place right there. She saw herself ride up in a white horse-drawn carriage. That was almost ten years before she even met Sean. I can only imagine that her vision right now is of just that.

"Will I need a bra?"

"I have no idea. If you do, I bet Beka brought one with her."

"That I did." Beka hangs the dress in its huge pink plastic bag over the top of the door. "Let's push the bed to the wall so we have more room." She looks around. "I hope this room is big enough."

Katie's surprised look makes me laugh.

"Off with the clothes." Beka hands me a strapless bra from a shopping bag while Katie removes her camisole. She sets a pair of white silk open-toed heels on the bed.

"These shoes are *Christian Louboutin*. They must have cost you a fortune." I run my hand over the silk toe.

Beka chuckles. "Actually, they were free. Leftovers from a runway show by an obscure Italian designer who I just happened to have a little fling with."

"A fling? A fling you didn't tell us about? Tell us more," I beg.

"There's nothing to tell. We spent one night together, I got a five hundred dollar pair of shoes. He's back in Milan already."

Katie's eyes widen into circles. "Night?"

"Yes, night of nights, night of dreams. Champagne, expensive hotel, room service, rose petals on satin sheets, and no strings. There's no more to tell except that the sex was outrageous."

"Outrageous?" Katie gulps. "You mean like a prostitute? Like he gave you a five hundred dollar pair of shoes to have sex with him? Now, you want me to wear them on my wedding day?"

Beka howls. "No. The shoes were worn on the runway. They got left behind by some designer's intern or one of the suppliers. Marcello struck up a conversation by telling me that Louboutin was obsessed with both shoes and the famous music halls of Paris. He said that besides feathers, the dancers wore virtually nothing except shoes. It was the combination of a naked body in a pair of shoes that first interested him in designing shoes."

The paling-by-the-second look on Katie's face makes me smile. "So, that was his pick up line?"

"Not exactly, well, maybe."

"What? Tell us?" I'm feeling as much out of breath as Katie.

Beka sighs. She knows better than to not tell us the whole truth. "We'd flirted earlier and then the shoes were an in for him, I guess. He offered them to me before he asked me to dinner, before we slept together. The shoes were free. They don't even fit me. I accepted them when I realized they were Katie's size. I knew they'd go beautifully with the gown."

"Oh," Katie smiles shyly. "I didn't mean to—"

"Not to worry. I guess it did sound like I got paid."

"Please tell us more," I say. "What do you mean about the sex being outrageous?"

"I'm not going to draw you a picture. Maybe...urgent, frantic, scrumptious. Like the richest dessert you can imagine. Something you can only handle once a year. Not something you'd want every day."

"Why did you keep this from us?" I slap my hands on my hips as if I'm admonishing her.

"When have I ever kept anything from you? No, I'm telling you now. It was just night before last. I wanted to tell you in person." Beka begins to remove Katie's gown from the plastic bag. "Close your eyes, Katie. We'll dress you. I don't want you to see the gown until you see yourself in it. Go on...close them. I promise that you won't be disappointed."

I take hold of Katie's shoulders from behind to steady her while Beka gently unfastens the line of tiny pearl buttons that extend from mid-back to tailbone.

While helping Katie into the tulle slip Beka looks deep into my eyes. "Weddings are for you and Katie, not me. Men like Marcello are for me. That's all I want or all I need. I'm feeling so satisfied, so fulfilled, so complete. I don't want to be tied down. Not yet."

"Tied down?" Katie almost shouts. "How can you say that?"

"I'm sorry, Katie. Maybe the right man just hasn't come along for me." Beka stares into my eyes.

"What?" I mouth the word.

Beka shrugs. "Maybe I'm waiting for the jazz singer."

"The jazz singer? What jazz singer?" Katie looks perplexed. "You mean Harry Connick, Jr."

"No, no, no. The movie, *The Jazz Singer*, remember?"

"You aren't talking about—what's his name—Neil, Neil Diamond, are you?" Katie asks.

"No way. Yussel Rabinowitz, the character in the movie, you know, someone too good to be true."

Katie and I burst out laughing. "Beka, Yussel was a cantor," I say. "Since when are you interested in a holy man?"

"He's just a dream man, I guess. I love that movie as much as my mom does. We watch it every time I come home. It's ingrained in my mind. Anyway, Yussel is just someone safe to romanticize about. Besides, I need time to get my career going, really going. I don't want to be obscure and have to work for someone else for the rest of my life. I want my own line of haute couture. Rebekah Schultzberg needs to stand shoulder-to-shoulder with *House of Chanel, Ralph Lauren, Versace*, even. I have to prove myself against these greats."

"That's why you went to the best schools. Your internship with *Vera Wang* wasn't a fluke. You got it because you showed talent and promise. You'll make it, Beka. You will."

A grin shows on her face as she continues dressing Katie but I also see a little wrinkle across her forehead. When the last button is fastened, Beka whispers, "Open your eyes."

Katie stands staring at her reflection in a ceramic silence. My mind races. All kinds of scenarios flash before me including the possibility that she doesn't like it. If she doesn't, what will she do? What will her not liking it do to Beka? Before I can stop my mind, Katie's hands fly to cover her face. "Beka. It's awesome. It's wonderful. It's so *me*." Tears splash down her cheeks like a flash flood.

Beka grabs a box of tissues from the bureau. "Don't tear-stain it before I can get pictures—for my portfolio. That is, if it's alright."

"Of course it is. I feel like a queen." Katie asks for the hand mirror on the dresser so she can see the back. "How did you know, Beka? I mean how did you do it? How did you create the most perfect gown? I feel like it's an extension of *me*. It's the best gift I've ever gotten. I can never thank you for this."

Beka did, indeed, outdo herself. The silk sweetheart bodice with modest capped sleeves and a snug princess style waist bursts into an organza skirt caught-up with the palest shell-pink satin roses. The look is soft, summery, and as contemporary as the attendant's gowns, yet would have been a welcomed addition to even the Baroness Pontalba's wardrobe of 1844. I look to Beka. "These gowns you've created—there's nothing like them in the bridal magazines. How do they rate on the scale of haute couture?"

"They won't rate very high now but with any luck, I'll at least get noticed, get my name out there. It's a tough business."

While we talk, Katie swirls like a dancing fairy on a spring morning. She can't take her eyes off her reflection in the mirror.

"I'm so happy for you, Katie." I can't get over the way she's glowing. "You're going to be the most radiant bride ever."

"It's gorgeous. I'm gorgeous. Look at the roses. You made them, didn't you? How will Sean control himself when he sees me walking down the aisle?"

"Katie." Beka shouts. "What's gotten into you?"

"I've never had a dress that made me look so, so—"

Beka cups a hand behind her ear, listening for Katie's response.

"Desirable, I guess." Katie just grins. No blushing. She's a picture of sheer radiance.

"How should I wear my hair? Do I need a veil or a wreath of flowers or what?"

"I'm leaving that up to you. We can look at options online. I'd suggest a simple shoulder-length veil without too much razzle-dazzle. The dress makes quite a statement but the focal point is still your face. People should remember what you looked like, not what the gown looked like."

While Beka walks around Katie, examining the gown, Katie's expression turns serious. "Beka, I hope someday you'll find someone like Sean or Zack. I don't know about outrageous sex but there's absolutely nothing better than falling asleep in the arms of someone who loves you dearly."

"You're right, Cinderella." Beka tilts her head. "But I'm not out there looking for Prince Charming. I'm waiting for someone to find me. If that doesn't happen, I won't be sad— at least I don't think I will be. Besides, we're twenty-five, not forty-five. I guess I'm just not ready."

"Katie's right, you know, Beka. You've done so well. Someday Katie and I can say our gowns were from the first wedding collection of the famous designer, Rebekah Schultzberg."

Beka rolls her eyes and swings her hair letting it fall to rest over one shoulder. "Let's get Katie out of this gown then I'll show you sketches of what I have in mind for you. I hope you won't think it's too simple after seeing Katie's."

Back at the dining room table, Beka takes in another great breath before she hands me a paper with four sketches. The gown is similar to the style for my bridesmaid's. The corset bodice is heavily beaded as is a front pleat that makes the skirt more elegant. My eyes shift from sketch to sketch. How did she do it? This dress is more me than me. I try but can't make a sound. Tears drip onto the page. I can't wait for Zack to see me in this gown, can't wait to walk down the aisle, can't wait until after the wedding when he'll tenderly unlace the corset to run his hands down my sides as the dress falls to the floor.

"Shelli?" Beka speaks softly. "What do you think?"

"It's gorgeous. I wish that my wedding was tomorrow. I can't wait to wear this dress. It's too perfect, much more perfect than I ever dreamed it could be." I press the sketches to my chest and feel a mystical union with Beka. "Did I ever tell you how much I love you?"

Both Beka and Katie come to my side with so much love overflowing. I feel the warmth of their bodies against mine.

A stabbing fear hits me—the first twinge of separation. The three of us are still the slobber sisters. Will Zack and Sean come between us? Our lives are about to change forever. I'm sobbing now, sobbing out of joy, sobbing out of impending doom. No, I shout in my head. The three of us will only grow stronger. We'll grow stronger because of the love from our husbands. There will be more than enough love. There will be. There has to be.

## 3

In mid-August, 2010 I sat on my vanity stool, looking at my reflection in the mirror, hoping that my mother couldn't read my devious mind.

A Midsummer Night's Dance at Chapel Hill High was my first high school dance. While getting ready that night my mother seemed to sense that she would lose her little girl forever. Maybe it was more my guilt than my mother's anxiety that caused my fingers to twitch like I was playing an invisible piano.

While Mama brushed my hair, she gave me a spiel on the birds and the bees. She didn't want boys getting their hands into my hair or any other place for that matter. Even though she had no tangible reason, she didn't trust the high school boys.

"I'll be careful." I told her as I went to the closet to slip into my favorite outfit—a sundress the color of the inside of a watermelon and a matching pair of faux crystal-studded flip-flops.

"You just became a woman last year. You know what can happen to you now."

"Yes, Mama, I know." As I returned to the stool, my lovely Zack flashed across my mind. Tonight would be *the* night. We'd been planning it for a month.

I watched my mother's reflection as she twisted my hair atop my head. I'd been excited about my plans but a sudden unexpected remorse that I was about to disobey my parents in the worst possible way threatened my anticipation. My mother was extremely trusting and I had a long leash. I knew I was taking advantage of both. When the style suited her, Mama fastened a pink banana clip snugly in place. She stopped to caress my shoulders. Love radiated down to my toes.

"Thanks, Mama," I choked out, willing myself not to let a single tear slip from my eye. I wanted to share my happiness with her. I wanted her to be waiting to hear all about everything, even the tiniest detail when I'd burst through the living room door in a few hours. But that would not happen. Even if things went horribly wrong, I wouldn't be able to look to her for comfort.

I didn't know then that I was a change of life baby. My mother was forty-three when I was born. My brother, Mordie, was sixteen, and my sister, Saphira, fifteen. By the time I was five, Mordie was a year away from graduating pre-med and Saphira was married to Rabbi Warren's son, Sol, so it was as if I were an only child. While I don't regret what I did on that sultry August night, I knew how much Mama's heart would ache if she ever found out.

Mama frowned when I smeared color across my lips. "Come, say goodbye to your father," she said, her tone just a bit disapproving.

Daddy looked up from his computer screen when I walked into his study. Musty books overflowed mahogany shelves and sat in stacks on an Oriental carpet. A green library lamp lit up a heavily highlighted paper at his elbow.

"My little girl is growing up much too fast to please me. Here," he said, "take the camera. Take lots of pictures so we can remember."

I smiled at my father wondering just what I might photograph. "I have my iPhone," I said. "It takes good pictures."

"Alright. Just remember to think—"

"I will, Daddy." I kissed his cheek. "Mama already went down the list."

"Well then, better get going. Don't want to keep Beka and Katie waiting. I'll pick you up at ten-thirty."

"Thanks, Daddy. I love you."

"Yes, yes, I love you too, my little *shayneleh*, my little pretty one."

"Let's go, Mama." I smiled at my father. His trust so evident that I felt even more guilty.

"Just be—"

"Careful. I will, Daddy. I will."

My heart pounded when Beka, Katie, and I got out of the car. As soon as Mama was out of sight I removed the banana clip and swished my hair from side to side letting it fall softly over my shoulders.

"Hey, Shelli."

"Zack." I looked down, giggling. Beka grabbed my phone, took a picture of Katie and me then one of Zack with me, then one of four of us. She handed the phone to Katie who took several more photos before sending them to my father's email.

"Thanks," I said when Katie returned my phone. "We'll meet you back here at ten twenty-nine sharp."

Katie smiled coyly. "Are you guys really going to do it? I mean go all the way, not just make out?"

I tried not to make eye contact with Zack. For the first time, I felt bashful. I couldn't figure out why because Katie's outburst wasn't unusual or unexpected.

"They probably will," Beka said. "Shelli promised to go first so she could tell us how to do it. You know how she always wants to be first. Especially this time."

"Why this time?" Katie wrinkled her nose.

"She doesn't want you to go first. She doesn't want to get beat by a Catholic."

"What's that supposed to mean?" Katie looked to me, eyebrows knitted.

"Catholic girls are known to be easy. They usually go first, then go to confession, say a few Hail Mary's. It's not so easy for us Jews to get atonement."

"Don't be silly. They're going to go all the way because they love each other. Right, Zack? Shelli said that if you're in love, it's not a sin to share your love."

"God help us." Beka rolled her eyes.

Zack took my hand. "Excuse us, ladies. Shelli and I have an appointment."

"In heaven," Katie shouted as Zack led me away. It was then I realized this would be our first time alone together.

Before we left the schoolyard, Zack stopped at the foot of the bleachers. He put his hands on the sides of my face, looked at me intently then kissed me. His mouth felt strangely cold. We'd made out lots of times over the past few months, sometimes pressing our bodies together but not long enough to extinguish our lustful desires. We met at the movies on Sunday afternoons. We always sat in the back row between Beka and Katie—our willing lookouts and decoys. *Someday*, I often told them, *I'll do the same for you.* Last week I'd let Zack run his hand up under my skirt. He touched the soft skin of my inner thigh but that's all. The week before that, I'd let him massage my breasts over my padded bra and T-shirt—but I didn't let him get under my shirt. More than once, he pressed my hand against his erection. I didn't know what to do. I tried to imagine what was under there making such a fuss. Our kisses were passionate, lasting the full length of the previews, film, and credits. But this only left us hungry for more.

"This is for you." Zack handed me a small, flat velvet box. "It's something to remind you of our first dance."

"We've danced together before." I held tightly to the box. "Oh." I gasped. "You didn't mean that kind of dancing did you?"

"No." He laughed. "I meant, at least I hope, it will remind you of our first time, you know—doing it together."

Inside the box was a gold heart-shaped locket. I opened it, but it was empty. Snapping it closed I felt a roughness on the back. I turned it over but couldn't read the engraving in the dim light.

"It's today's date." Zack had the look of a hopeful puppy at the pound.

"Thank you." I wrapped my sweaty palm around it. I felt excitement swirl through me until I thought I might puke— not from his sentimental gesture but from my anticipation and sudden anxiety. I asked Zack to fasten the necklace at the back of my neck. "I don't think I'll ever forget the date," I said, forcing each word. With the donning of the locket, I felt a twinge of obligation, although I really didn't need to be prodded. Still, I wondered if the engraved locket meant that I had to do it, that I had to go all the way, even if everything didn't feel right at the last moment. There seemed to be no turning back, no way out now, even if I'd wanted out—which I didn't think I did. Maybe Zack thought he might lose his nerve if he didn't give me the keepsake prior to our private encounter.

"Let's go." Zack took my hand. "Everything's ready."

The walk to Zack's backyard was a quick one. We didn't speak. We just squeezed hands.

"We have a good two hours," Zack said, urging me up the ladder. His treehouse hadn't been occupied in almost four years. He'd cleaned it up, he'd said, even dusted and stashed candles, matches, and condoms inside a rolled-up sleeping bag. "My folks won't be home until after eleven. Their movie lets out at nine-forty and then they'll go to the Martini Bar uptown for a few drinks."

Zack unrolled the sleeping bag. I could see a smile on his face when he lit the first candle. "You were the prettiest girl at the dance."

"The prettiest or the luckiest?"

"What do you mean?" Zack sat us down on the rolled out sleeping bag. He smelled clean, like the soap in a ritzy hotel bathroom.

"I think I'm the luckiest girl in the world to be here with—"

Zack covered my mouth with his. The kiss was warm this time. I felt him pulling me into him. Angst filled me. I felt as if I was slipping away, as if he was pulling the life out of me. I wasn't certain that I wanted to be there. I felt limp, lifeless, weightless. I feared I might pass out. Zack eased me to lie back. He looked at me with such tenderness that my fears dissolved. He slipped the spaghetti strap off my shoulder then reached inside my dress to touch my breast.

"I can feel your heartbeat. I love you, Shelli."

I wasn't certain what to do next. His palm felt warm. I welcomed it by pushing myself up into his hand. I knew he loved me. I wanted him to love me. I wanted him to make love to me. My life, at that moment, depended upon it.

He kissed me hard with more passion than before. I got lost in it. Before I knew it, we were completely undressed, pressing our skin together. I was out of my body by then— gone far away into a fairytale, lost in pleasure and delight. Then he rolled me over. Before my mind could catch up with my physical passions, we'd done it.

Our lovemaking was desperate, frantic. We both lost our virginity easily with just a quick sting and one short-lived salty tear. My body shook with excitement. Zack pulled me to him. He held me tightly, kissing my face and hair until my shaking ceased. We lay together listening to the symphony of the cicadas that hid in the night. Zack buried his face in my hair. I thought I heard a sniffle. Neither of us spoke for the longest time. Then we lost ourselves in each other again. The second time lasted longer. I was more aware of the blissful state we were in. Zack rolled us to our sides while we remained connected physically. We held to each other for dear life. Happiness filled me to the brim making me want to run all the way home to tell Mama all about everything but knew I couldn't share this with her. I couldn't share it with anyone. So, I folded up the precious memories and tucked them away inside my new locket, close to my heart forever.

We didn't say the words out loud until years later but we both knew that we'd been led to this spot, on this night, by divine power. What we'd done had to be sacred in God's eyes. What we'd done couldn't be misconstrued as sinful or evil, even though we'd been led to this place by our youthful, biological urges and lustful desires. We knew little of love before this total sharing of our bodies but afterward, we were bound together in some calm security that would surely continue into eternity. Our first dance made love real. It turned love into something we could grasp and understand. It helped us appreciate our parent's cautious concerns for us, as well as the reasons people risked their own lives, not only for those they love but also for total strangers in some desperate need. We contemplated love in all its complexities. Each time we spoke the word, we bonded more tightly into one.

## 4

Over the years love has become synonymous with life—everything is simply better because of it. Jealousy, the evil we watched rip so many of our friends' relationships apart, has never entered our lives. Zack and I find our bond to be tighter because we enable each other to be unique while we enjoy our individual passions. Case in point—last week UNC won their third basketball game in a row. Since the boys were still celebrating the victories, Katie and I decided on a girls' night out.

When I arrive at Katie's to pick her up for our night on the town I'm surprised by a house packed with friends. Once inside, I see that Katie has decorated her townhouse to the hilt with all the glorious colors of my wedding. A bridal shower. I'm totally amazed but have to say that another celebration of the latest Tar Heel win seemed a bit much.

There's so much to take in as I'm warmly greeted by so many smiling friends.

Katie calls everyone to attention by tapping a spoon on a wine glass. I know from the way she's smiling that something's up.

To my delight, I spot Beka in the den surrounded by all six of my bridesmaid's gowns on papier-mâché dress forms. Seeing the gowns together makes me wilt. My love for Beka and the reality of her genius overcome me. Beka hugs me tightly. Over her shoulder, I spot Mama standing beside a table filled with an assortment of my favorite ethnic cuisine—cheese blintzes with strawberry jam, honey cakes, macaroons, a cinnamon babka, even a chocolate charm cake with so many ribbons protruding that there must be a fortune message for every guest. I can tell by the proud look on Mama's face that she's prepared all of it just to please me.

My mother has always been there for me, no matter how far I stray from her heart. I make my way to embrace her.

"I'm going to be Zack's wife but I'll always be your daughter, always."

"I know." She presses her lips together into a straight line as she dabs at my tears with the corner of a tissue. "You're going to have two mothers now," she says as she reaches out to Zack's mother.

Mrs. Levy looks so young compared to Mama but that's probably because she's just a couple years older than my sister. I barely know Zack's mother. She hugs me lightly. The embrace leaves moisture on my cheek. I notice that her eyes are red-rimmed. "You look beautiful," I say, feeling uneasy, wondering as to her emotion. "I'm so pleased you're here."

"Thank you. You're the beautiful one, darling." Mrs. Levy smiles as tears trickle down her cheeks. "Enjoy your party. We'll talk later."

The complexities of her mixed emotions confuse me. When I squeeze her hand, I feel a spark of something good between us. I want to say something more but I hear the music of a violin playing *Mayim Mayim,* my favorite Hebrew folksong from childhood. Everyone is clapping and smiling now. Mama pushes me through the crowd to the bottom of the stairs. I look up to see my sister, Saphira, dressed in a black spaghetti-strap dress that hugs her trim frame. She reminds me of the stylish Catherine, Duchess of Cambridge, or maybe more of her sister, Pippa. She descends the stairs gracefully in three-inch strappy heels. Mama holds me back, keeps me from running up the stairs to greet her.

When she reaches the bottom step, we hug and squeal with delight. We haven't seen each other since I left med school last term. Before I can catch my breath I hear my nieces call my name. I turn to see the two of them followed by their mother, my sister-in-law, Rachel. They have dressed alike in sheer tea length, pastel dresses over pink satin slips. They throw themselves at me. I can't hold back tears as I squeeze them until they're giggling wildly.

The shock of Naomi's physical condition devastates me. Even though I'd heard how quickly she'd gone downhill, I didn't believe it until now. She's emaciated with deep shadows around sunken dark eyes that once held so much light. I hadn't expected all this from a girl with a brain tumor the size of a piece of rice. Yesterday, my brother Mordie called to let me know they'd given Naomi a diagnosis— Neurofibromatosis Type 2. It's rare—only affects one in forty thousand. Some of her symptoms don't fit. Mordie says there's not much research literature out there. Not all his medical training can make him the kind of doctor who can save his child from the wrath of death. I doubt the diagnosis but seeing her in this ghastly condition confirms my worst fears.

Katie clinks her spoon against a wine glass again as Beka shouts, "Mazel tov. Let's eat, drink, and be merry."

I hug Rachel who appears to be hiding her anxiety behind her smile. "I know," I say. She hugs me tighter, we both swallow tears. Neither of us wants to let go until Beka brings us wine, gingerly balancing the tray on her fingertips.

"Something you learned in New York?" I ask to tease her.

"This and more," she says as she pours garnet wine into crystal glasses. "I'm serving a Roberto Cohen Sancerre 2001, a robust kosher French red from the esteemed Loire Valley."

"Well done. I'm impressed." I smile at Rachael as Beka walks to the next group.

"We're here to celebrate you," Rachael says. "Not to grieve."

Naomi has her arms glued around my legs. I tousle her hair. I sip the wine, think about the last time I saw her, before this wretched demon entered her. I see her dark brown eyes with their long black lashes framed by thick ponytails tied up in ribbons and silk flowers—a little girly-girl, dressed in a prissy dress. She could hop endlessly on one foot. My jaw clenches. What if she doesn't make it?

I give Naomi a special look. She lets go of my legs. I take her hand in mine, let her warm my heart with her loving eyes, her bony moist hand. I say a prayer for her. *Don't leave us, Naomi. Stay here where you are loved. Stay where you are treasured. Stay. Let us watch you grow up.* Her fate isn't in my hands, I know that but I can't give her up. I want to yell at her to be strong as though it's up to her to make herself well. I smile instead. She smiles back and then turns and raises her arms for Rachel to hold her. I purposely don't make eye contact with Rachael but I touch her arm. Mama leads me away, back into the celebration.

Mama keeps close to me, one arm around my waist, the other resting on my hip closest to her as if she's displaying a treasure or protecting me from falling. My heart swells. I've felt this before but never like I'm feeling it now. My mother is showing me off, raising me up, loving me with all her heart. I stand straighter, hold my head higher. I fight back tears. Not tears of happiness, tears of sadness.

To Mama, I am the ideal daughter. When Zack and I moved in together, Mama alone supported me, even though I knew I was breaking her heart. She wanted me to be a virgin on my wedding night, same as she had been, same as Saphira had been. The one secret that stood between us, the one that probably would have ruined our mother-daughter bond was the knowledge that I'd freely given my virginity away years before Zack and I decided to cohabitate.

The sounds around me turn into a distant hum as I realize just how much I am loved. Instantly I decide to transform my union with Zack into a sacred expression of the faith of my parents and sister and brother, not the secular social gathering I had, until this moment, envisioned. This decision will please my family. I owe it to them. But more than that I want to let them share in the celebration of my union with Zack. Chills zing down my spine. Finally, I am at peace, atoned, and one with my mother, the dearest woman in the world.

By the end of the evening, when all the oohs and ahhs, hugs, and thank-yous are memories, I feel overwhelmed in a melancholy sort of way. Katie, Beka, and Mama have outdone themselves. I find it hard to believe that all this outpouring of love is for me. Sean brought Zack in at the end of the party. After a round of introductions, the two of them escaped to the patio with plates of food and a couple bottles of beer. Beka, Katie, and I sit on the couch, me in the middle, with our legs propped up on the coffee table.

I lean back and revel in a multitude of cherished memories.

Beka squeezes my hand. "Are you still with us, dream girl?"

"Sorry. I was just thinking about how content I am."

"It was good to see Saphira and Rachael." Katie sighs. "Your whole family is successful. It's impressive."

"Yeah, one family with three doctors and a rabbi in it." Beka shakes her head. "So my family is Jewish already?"

"Two doctors," I say. "I still have a year to go, which brings us to something important."

*"Oy vay.* That mind of yours never stops."

"I was just thinking about my wedding."

"You still want to do it, don't you?" Katie sits up straight, whips her head around to look at me.

"Of course I do. But not the way I planned." I fold my arms across my chest.

"What then?" Beka asks, her eyes searching mine.

I look through the sliding glass door. Zack and Sean are trying to play one-on-one basketball on the modest patio. "I'm sure Zack will go for it but I need to talk with you guys before I get too carried away."

"Tell us. What's going on?" Beka looks to Katie then back to me.

"I'm feeling a little emotional right now. Did you notice how Mama stuck so close to me? And Zack's mom? She looked like she was about to break down. It wasn't until halfway through the party that I remembered Zack's sister, Emma. I got the feeling that although Zack's mom is happy about Zack marrying me, she's missing Emma, missing Emma's wedding."

"Oh no. I'd forgotten all about Emma." Katie presses her knuckles to her lips.

"How many times tonight did we toast *to life?*" Beka asks. "Oh Shell. Damn."

I remember the day I turned sixteen, the day my parents officially allowed me to date. I introduced Zack to my parents. He was acceptable to them, even if his family was Reform and in spite of his protestant mother who converted to Judaism, yet continued to put up a Christmas tree in the front window every December. After all, Mama thought, we were young—not to worry about a serious future. My parents knew there'd be many orthodox young men in my future—just like there had been for Saphira. Still, they had a soft spot for Zack, the tall brunette, hazel-eyed boy who seemed to need them as much as he needed me.

In Zack's first few visits to our home, my parents badgered him with questions about himself, his plans for college, his family. They crowned him an official suitor when they learned that his only sibling, Emma, just two years younger than Zack, died from leukemia when she was eleven. Although both were successful in the community and quite affluent, it was widely known that alcohol had saved them from the depression following Emma's death. They became heavy drinkers. The late afternoon ritual of martinis or scotch on the rocks, one after the other, became their mainstay.

"No wonder Mrs. Levy was so teary. God."
Both Beka and Katie startle at my outburst.
"What?" Beka asks.

"Mrs. Levy asked if I'd wear her pearl necklace. Mr. Levy's mother gave it to her when she converted just before they married. It was supposed to become a family tradition—to hand the pearls down from mother to daughter but, well, Emma died too soon."

"You said you would, didn't you?" Tears brim Katie's eyes.

"Of course, I did. I told her I'd be honored. She caught me completely off guard. She's still grieving for Emma, the daughter who never got to grow up, the daughter who never got to have a wedding. Her heart is aching, I think. I can see it in her eyes."

"Isn't she putting pressure on you, Shelli? I mean—"

"It's okay, Beka. I think it's more an honor. Emma should have worn the pearls—not me. It must have been difficult for her to hand them down."

"Sounds like she needs you to be more than a daughter-in-law." Beka bites her bottom lip.

"If I'm going to carry on a tradition, I might as well go all the way."

"Like how, what?" Katie asks with a confused expression.

"Like the whole orthodox thing." I take in a deep breath. "I've broken so many family traditions, made decisions without consulting my parents, yet they're all still here beside me, supporting me. I want to involve them in the wedding. Make their dreams for me come true. Will you help?"

"Like you need to ask?" Beka's smile reassures me.

"I'll run it by Zack tonight. Then break the news to Mama tomorrow morning. We'll have to rush things. The wedding is just nine weeks away. Do you think we can pull it off?"

"Like pros." Beka says, giving Katie a high-five.

"I'm so lucky having you two schlemiels for best friends."

On our way home, I broach the subject with Zack, try to convince him that our wedding should be about our mothers' dreams for us. This sentiment is as new to Zack as it was to me a few hours ago. I let him examine the idea before I rush to announce my new plan. If it was up to Zack we'd elope to some tropical island and say our "I dos" to a Justice of the Peace with me in a sarong and him in shorts with an open sports shirt. I feel nervous and emotional all of a sudden. Zack slows the car to a stop along the side of the road. "What about our mothers' dreams?" he asks.

"The service—it needs to be serious." I hesitate. "It needs to be…traditional."

Zack looks at me. I sense he's looking through me, sorting things out. I know better than to interrupt.

After a long silence, I can no longer contain my thoughts. I tell him about the new insight I have into my mother, his mother, Emma, the pearls. I tell him that every mother dreams of her daughter's wedding and every father hopes that his daughter will marry a man who will cherish her as much he does. I tell him that I've changed my mind because of all that's happened in the past few hours. I ask if he'll let our parents celebrate us."

"As much as I'm going to regret saying this, you're probably right." A shrewd smile covers Zack's face. "There'll be conditions."

"What's that? I'll do anything."

"Just what a horny man wants to hear." Zack lets out a little chuckle. "How about a little extra excitement in bed for, let's see, a week, a month?"

"You rat."

"Take it or leave it, my darling."

"You are the biggest spoiled brat in the universe."

"I thought you said I was a rat."

"Start the car, you bratty rat's ass," I say laughing. "Thank you, Zack."

"Whatever the lady wants, the—"

"Will you go with me to tell my parents and yours tomorrow morning?"

"Can't." Zack's smile is smug. "I'm teeing off at ten with Sean."

"Well, then, you'll have to cut our morning activities a little short, Mr. Levy."

"I thought you were asking."

"If you want a great performance tonight you'd better roll that tush out of bed early. We're expected for coffee at both my parents' house and yours tomorrow morning. I have to pick up Katie and Beka by ten anyway."

As we pull into the driveway Zack asks, "What devious plans have you three cooked up?"

My smile is broad. I raise my eyebrows. "We're going to plan an orthodox wedding."

## 5

After Zack and I have incredible sex, I lie awake remembering the summer after we graduated high school. We decided not to miss the total college experience by staying monogamous. Our strong foundation and uncanny trust was certain to sustain our love. I was off to pre-med at The University of Virginia in Charlottesville while Zack had his eyes set on Georgia Tech where he would major in industrial design. After graduation, the splendor of the Carolina clear blue sky lured Zack back to Chapel Hill where he earned a Masters of Business Administration at UNC but my sights were set on the big city. I began medical school at Mt. Sinai School of Medicine in Manhattan.

Zack settled into the job of his dreams at Ethan Yeager Enterprises, an international firm in Research Triangle Park, specializing in research-based telecommunication products design and development. The next year he bought a new three-bedroom townhouse in Meadowmount—a community on Highway 54 in Chapel Hill with a straight shot into RTP. Since I would be living there with him someday, he garnered my assistance in decorating and furnishing it. Other than investing in a good bed, we bartered for everything else at yard sales, thrift shops, and antique shops. It hadn't been easy for either of us to be apart once we'd turned the townhouse into our little love nest.

My second year at Mt. Sinai proved to be more demanding than the first. I'd stayed in the city over the Christmas break to work on an important project that was due the first week in January. I'd wanted to spend the break in Chapel Hill but I'd fallen far behind in my research. On the day before New Year's Eve, I could finally see the vision of the project take shape. I knew that if I kept pushing myself the assignment could be completed before the deadline. The phone startled me from my stacks of research and textbooks.

"Shelli. It's me, Saphira. You have to do something for me. Are you free?"

"I'm up to my forehead in research. What's up?"

"Is that black cocktail dress Beka gave you clean?"

"Yes. Do you need to borrow it?"

"No. Listen very carefully. Put it on. There's a cab waiting for you with the number 2J864 on the roof. See you soon. Hurry."

My mind went blank. I peered between the louvered shades to see a cab with its emergency flashers on. "What the...?" I pulled off my sweats, splashed water under my arms, washed my face, donned the dress and a pair of black velvet pumps then switched to a sexier Stiletto imitation with crisscross straps. I ran a brush through my hair, grabbed a lipstick, all the paper cash I had, my driver's license, keys, phone and threw them into an evening bag. I was halfway down the hall before turning back to get my coat. When I stepped into the cab, I wondered what in the heck I was doing.

The cabbie let me off in front of *Daniel*, a French restaurant on Manhattan's Upper East Side. When I pulled out some cash he told me that the bill had been paid.

I walked into the majestic foyer. Tiny crystals rained down from a brass chandelier. The maître d', in white tie and tails, gently touched my elbow. "Ms. Segal?"

"Yes."

*"Bonsoir*, Mademoiselle. Follow me, *s'il vous plaît."*

I was led through a dimly lit central hallway lined with golden silk drapes that spilled onto thick maroon carpets. Ornate, wingback chairs and small tables with lamps were arranged in groups. It looked more like a room that people simply walk through. The formal dining room was bright from the glow of a multitude of crystal chandeliers, a lively contrast from the muted entrance and hallway. It was after ten and the place was buzzing with men in three-piece suits or tuxedos sitting with women in jeweled gowns. The maître d' stopped at a small, canopied table for two in the back corner and pulled out a chair. I sat, feeling quite conspicuous. A waiter poured water into a crystal goblet. My heart pounded as I looked down at my shaking hands wondering where Saphira was and what we would do in a place like this. A man cleared his throat as he approached. I looked from my hands to a pair of black wingtips then up the legs of a charcoal silk suit to a Carolina blue tie. "Zack."

Zack stood before me, rocking from one foot to the other, with his hands behind his back. The look on his face was forlorn as if he was about to tell me that he was dying of cancer or something.

"What is it?" My hands began to sweat. I reached out for him.

"Shell, I can't live without you. I can't. I've tried, believe me, I have." He offered me a long white box tied up in a deep green satin ribbon.

I opened it to find a dozen watermelon and yellow zinnias. I inhaled their lemony sweetness. "They're beautiful. Thank you but…"

"You're welcome. They're not as beautiful as you."

"Sit, Zack." I reached out for him as tears erupted. "I love you. You know that. Don't you?"

Zack slipped into a chair and scooted it close to mine so that our thighs touched. He wiped my tears with his thumb. "This living alone in a house I hope to one day share with you is killing me. I've tried to date—it doesn't work, not even for fun. If I take a girl out and things progress to the bedroom, I feel as if I'm using her or betraying you or both. Shelli, I came here to ask you to marry me." Zack slid off his chair and knelt on one knee beside me. "Will you be my wife?"

I threw my arms around his neck. We kissed deeply as applause erupted around us and a flash went off. "I thought we'd decided that nine years ago," I said, nearly choking on my words.

"We did. But I want to make it official. I want to marry you tonight or tomorrow morning or next week or in the summer. Please marry me. I love you more than life."

"Yes, Zack, yes. I've always wanted you—never anyone else. Never."

"Then will you wear this?" Zach reached into his pocket, pulled out an aqua box tied up in a white ribbon.

I just held onto the little blue Tiffany box. "Oh Zack."

"Open it." He was smiling now and still on his knee.

The diamond, perched royally in a gold Edwardian setting, couldn't have been more perfect. Zack removed it from the box then slipped it on my left ring finger.

"It's gorgeous." I stared at the sparkling brilliance, swept away for a moment, until Zack covered my mouth with his. The waiter interrupted our passion and Zack returned to his chair.

"Look." I held out my hand. "We've just become engaged."

The waiter looked as if he should be working a café on the Champs-Elysées with his slicked-back hair, white dress shirt, black vest, and long, white apron wrapped snuggly over black trousers. He bowed. *"Félicitations* to the handsome couple." he said with a heavy French accent before completing a military about-face and walking away.

When I caught my breath I looked at Zack and said, "You won't believe this…last summer I applied for a transfer to Duke."

"What? You did? Because of me?" Zack touched his heart.

"I feel the same as you about the new townhouse. I want to live there with you."

"Think about it, Shell. We've lived apart for almost six years. I'm ready to settle down, ready to do the husband thing. I want to give you more than a diamond ring. I want to be a good husband—like my father and yours. I want to love you the way they love our mothers."

"That's the sweetest thing you've ever said." My arms went limp. I could barely raise them to brush tears from the corners of my eyes.

"I mean it, Shell. I can't wait—I don't want to wait any longer."

"Me either but I have two more years of med school after this one." I pressed my hand into Zack's thigh. "Our plan was to get married as soon as I finish."

"I know but now that we're engaged…Hey, what about Duke? Why didn't you tell me?"

"Duke has the top-of-the-line neurology and neurosurgery departments. If I want to specialize, I'll need that state-of-the-art program. I didn't say anything because I didn't want to get your hopes up if I'm rejected."

"When will you know?"

"I've been preliminarily accepted but there's no space for me unless someone drops out. I wouldn't want anyone to fail but someone might change specialties or schools. That's what I'm counting on."

"How likely is it?"

I shook my head. "If a space opens for me at Duke, I'll open a space for someone else here. It's as easy as that. A domino effect. No one has to drop out or fail…just move on."

"That's a positive way to look at it." Zack smiled. "If you get accepted you'll have to leave Beka and Saphira and her family too. How do you feel about that?"

"I rarely see Beka. She's busier than me. Both our schedules are horrendous. We talk on the phone mostly anyway and we can do that just as easily if I'm in North Carolina. Besides, Katie is back home now. I want to spend time with her. Saphira is another story. I'll miss her terribly but I cherish this time I've had with her, Sol, and my nephews. I'm ready, Zack, ready to come home."

"This is more than I'd hoped for." Zack clasped his hands behind his head. A satisfied grin grew into a wide smile. His mission was accomplished.

Thinking back on the years we spent apart, I think that the basis of our relationship—love and respect—remained intact when most relationships would have crumbled. We ran up huge phone bills telling each other about our sexual encounters. We arranged our trysts with each other at my parent's condo in Wilmington. I had sex with other guys because I knew Zack was having sex, not because I wanted it or was especially attracted to anyone. Zack was my one-and-only. I marked my dates up to experience. When I thought Zack was having too much fun, I'd arrange to meet him at my parent's condo at the beach. I didn't have much trouble separating sex for fun with other guys and making love to Zack. What I wasn't certain of was what was going on in Zack's world. The way he loved me at the condo should have been proof but then we were young and well, you never know about handsome jocks.

"You know that I've never had a romantic notion about anyone but you," Zack said. "The sex I had was purely recreational."

"That's what you always told me. What I always tried to believe. But what about that big boobed Jennifer what's her name?" I twist my engagement ring around my finger, reveling in it. "I have to say I was a little worried. You saw her a lot in your sophomore *and* junior year."

Zack let out a laugh. He leaned back until the front legs of the chair were off the ground. "There was nothing there except big, soft tits. We never went below the waist. She loved kissing and I loved squeezing those forty-double D's."

"Truth?"

"Truth."

"So, I should get a boob job?"

"Shelli, no. I love your body, just the way it is." He pulled at the plunging neckline of my dress and peeked inside. "I'd love to have those ladies in my hands right now."

"Well, don't worry. These ladies can wait at least until we get back to my apartment. Hey, I thought I was supposed to meet Saphira here."

"Our little surprise." Zack winked. "I didn't want you to worry about entertaining me or picking me up at the airport. So, I got a little help from your sister. She invited me to a party at a friend's apartment above Time's Square tomorrow. She's hoping you'll join us."

"You make me so happy, Zack."

The maître d' placed two flutes of champagne in front of us. "I hear congratulations are in order." He took a step back. "*Compliments de la maison*. Please, enjoy."

We lifted the flutes. "L'chaim." Zack said.


At the last minute, a space opened for me at Duke. Six months after our engagement, I moved into our little townhouse in Meadowmount. Even though Zack and I were already married in our hearts, we decided to move the wedding up a year to ease the pressure we'd put on ourselves by "living in sin" as my parents described it. At least we'd just live in sin for the next school year. I justified our co-habitation for the sake of my parents—with our engagement and commitment, Zack and I *were* married except for the little certificate from the government.


Getting married by a Justice of the Peace now seems so meaningless. Marriage is a sacrament in the eyes of my family. I'm just now realizing what a disappointment a secular ceremony would have been in their eyes. I think about that for a moment and realize that I'm not just doing this for them. I want this to be more than just tying the knot. I can hardly wait to make plans.

When I pull into Katie's drive, she and Beka are standing on the front porch waiting. I'd called them when we left my parents, and again after we left Zack's, so, they already know how excited everybody is. They'd spent half the night looking things up on the internet while I kept my promise to Zack.

Katie sits up front and Beka climbs into the seat behind her. We're headed to the library at the synagogue to make certain we plan the wedding correctly. Beka thinks they've figured out most of it, but we want to make certain we aren't planning something that will embarrass my family or the rabbis involved.

"Jewish weddings sure are more fun than Catholic ones," Katie says, as I back out on to the street.

"Tell me what you've come up with." I say with a shake of my head and a yawn.

"Are we keeping you awake?" Beka jiggles my ponytail.

"I was much too excited to sleep so I gave Zack the first hundred blow-jobs he'd demanded."

"What?" Katie blinks as the blood drains from her face. "He made you do it?"

"No, Katie." I smile at her. "It was our deal. He said he'd change the wedding plans if I'd give him...a little something extra in bed."

"He asked for a hundred..." Katie is flushed now.

Beka laughs. "She can't even say blow job. Come on, Katie, it's not even a four-letter word."

"Stop teasing her, Beka. I just made that up, the one hundred part. Zack was joking with me. So, what did you come up with? Where do we start?"

"If you want to go all the way, and I know you do," Beka snickers.

"Stop it, Beka." Katie's cheeks have turned crimson.

"I want everything. Mama and Saphira told me all about their weddings and I want mine to be as traditional and memorable as theirs."

"I think we can do it, Shelli," Katie says. "I learned so much about Jewish weddings last night and this morning that I wish I could have a Jewish wedding too."

The first thing we did was network. Beka had her laptop, Katie and I had iPads, and we all had smartphones. They showed me several Jewish wedding sites so I could get the general idea of where we wanted to go with this. We started with a Shabbaton—a whole weekend of traditional festivities both religious and social. Mama wanted to host the Friday night Shabbat dinner. We all agreed that this would give Zack and me a chance to socialize with our guests before the wedding, since they all told us that we'll be too emotional at the reception.

Saturday morning we'll schedule an aufruf at the synagogue. The groom is supposed to do the chanting before and after the Torah reading. I'm not sure Zack will go for that but one of his groomsmen, Barry Stein, is a cantor for a congregation in Miami. I'm sure he'll teach Zack to chant. The rabbi gives a special blessing to the bride and groom then the congregation throws candy and as Beka says, "Hopefully to shower you two with sweetness, not because of Zack's dreadful chanting."

Mrs. Levy volunteered to host the Kiddush luncheon Saturday afternoon in her backyard. We agreed that this would be a great idea since Mrs. Levy is used to entertaining large crowds. Zack and I would simply show up and not have to worry about the details.

"Listen to this." I read a line from a book on Jewish weddings about the tradition of the bride and groom separating for a week before the wedding to ready them to make their spiritual commitment public. "All this ritual is starting to make sense."

"Like how?" Beka looks up from a magazine article.

"The whole idea of a wedding is to make our spiritual commitment public. I like that. Besides, if we're not together for a week can you imagine the magic of seeing each other when we emerge from our separation at the Shabbat dinner? Oh my god. I'm totally going to get a new dress for that."

"Sounds romantic," Beka says and I catch the wink she sends my way, "but what are you supposed to do while you're apart?"

"It says here to fast, meditate, and reflect upon life and the gratitude you feel." Katie looks up. "Like write your own vows?"

"Yes. Zack and I already talked about doing that. Great thinking, Katie."

Beka cocks her head. "Then, maybe, you could both read them every day while you're apart. Would that work?"

"Yes, that would work." I visualize reading the vows, rising to another plane, to a place where Zack and I reside spiritually, to the place before time when we were once one.

Beka and I remember the traditional mikvah—a ritual bath to symbolize the bride's transformation from a single to a married woman. It's also a time to reconnect with the Divine Presence, something that I've lost over the years. My mikvah will be in the ocean, I decide, rather than in a tiled tub at the synagogue. Beka and Katie agree to accompany me to the beach.

This afternoon we're feeling pretty satisfied with our plans. As we pack up to leave, Katie finds one more thing— henna parties. She tells us that for thousands of years women in the Middle East and North Africa—Jewish, Muslim, and Christian alike—have had intricate designs painted on their hands and feet with henna before the wedding. "Let's do this," she says, holding up a finger. "It can be a fun celebration on Friday night after you separate from Zack. We can do it at my place then head to the beach on Saturday for your mikvah."

I feel almost indifferent to the idea. I'm already thinking of the seriousness of the other rituals. Why not? I remind myself that I wanted tradition but I also want fun.

As we pack up to leave, I know we have made the right choices. With Katie and Beka at my side, how can this huge undertaking fail?

## 6

A week before our wedding weekend, I kiss Zack goodbye for what will begin our separation. While studying Jewish traditions I learned that this time is important for us because it provides a time for both to reflect on our relationship and spend quality time with close friends and family. It also allows us to view our lives without each other. The rabbi suggested that we each hold our own ceremonies where we can be blessed by our friends and family. Katie's desire to host a henna party for me fit smack into this ritual.

When I pull up in front of Katie's townhouse, I see the glow of candlelight through the front window. Once inside I hardly recognize anyone. Five women, all in full tribal belly dance regalia, greet me. The sound of tribal drums and finger symbols adds to the mystique. All the furniture except the sofa has been removed. Several large pillows in bright earth colors cover the empty floor. The aroma of cinnamon, tea, and spices I can't identify not only fill my head but seem to penetrate my skin as well. Two copper trays are set beside the stacks of pillows—one filled with almonds, pistachio nuts, olives, and feta cheese, another with bowls of babaganoish and hummus surrounded by stacks of pita bread. A third tray offers pastries cut into bite-sized pieces including baklava, macaroons, and a cinnamon chocolate rugelach.

Katie, Beka, Mama, and Mrs. Levy dance around me while Yasmeen, a henna painter and belly dance instructor, introduces herself. She instructs me to remove my clothing so I can dress in garb similar to theirs. I don a pair of dark red harem pants and a black circle skirt with an embroidered hem. Yasmeen helps me into a bra covered in silver coins and a dark red vest that matches the pants. Mama ties a dark red scarf with tassels around my hips while Katie slips a silver Kuchi necklace over my head. Beka places silver bangles on my wrists while Yasmeen wraps a colorful turban around my head.

Everyone's face glows in the candlelight—Mama's with pride, Mrs. Levy's with acceptance, Beka's with love, Katie's with joy, Yasmeen's with satisfaction. When Yasmeen marks my eyes and chin with kohl and adds a bindi to the corner of each eye, the four of them cover their mouths and let out a loud high-pitched ululation.

"Look at you guys. You're gorgeous." I'm laughing with delight. "What's that sound?"

Yasmeen steps forward. "It's the zaghareet, the sound of celebration for weddings and other joyful occasions." She instructs me so I can join in with the others, even Mama who wasn't sure how we'd be treated by Yasmeen, a Muslim, Iranian-American.

The music changes to an instrumental Arabic Groove. Yasmeen teaches me a few basic belly dance moves and before long, I'm dancing with the others in a circle. We all repeat the zaghareet when someone gets a move right. I feel relaxed, sensual, and festive—a good beginning as I prepare for the week ahead.

"I don't think I could dance like this in street clothes," Mrs. Levy says with hips swaying. "These costumes make it so much easier." She smiles and I revel in it.

"Try this move, it's the hip shimmy." Yasmeen demonstrates. I laugh at the stunned look on Mama's face but she tries the move and does a good rendition.

Katie giggles while shaking her hips with her arms up over her head. "This is fun."

As the music changes again to a new beat, we let out more zaghareets. Soon we flop on to the floor to lounge on the overstuffed pillows and catch our breath.

Mama and Mrs. Levy seem to have bonded. I watch them talk and laugh as if they are girlfriends. I see a vision of

Katie, Beka, and me years into the future, chatting away with arthritic backs and grey hair. If a heart can smile, mine is.

While Yasmeen paints floral designs on our hands and feet, I have to act the part of the queen while everyone waits on me. We feast on the delicacies while Yasmeen tells stories about the bridal henna painting custom that has been handed down through generations of women. I feel a connection to these brides as if I'm being accepted into a sacred clan. I envision a tent filled with my ancestors thousands of years ago. I feel as if they've dreamed this moment into life.

My plan to include ancient rituals and scripture in my wedding binds me not only to my ancestors but to my mothers and sisters in this room. I feel blessed by a power greater than my own will. I am one with the universe. I am ready to begin the journey into my new life—a life of love for my husband, surrounded by strong women who will stand by me forever. It's time for me to fulfill my prophecy, not to please my mother or atone for my sins, but to step forward, with the help of an ancient heritage. I find my place in the here and now. I am a bride. As one phase of my life is ending, a new one is emerging. I am caught off guard emotionally. My wedding, so planned with rituals and scriptures, will be a reflection of Zack and me. The Almighty will sanctify and celebrate the love we share.

When we're exhausted from dancing and feasting, each one reads a blessing she has written for me. Katie pastes them into a little booklet that Yasmeen has decorated with the same designs she's painted on my hands.

Caught up in the moment, I stand to dance the dance of a bride, a dance I'm certain has been danced for five thousand years. A dance that will be repeated into eternity.

When Beka, Katie, and I arrive at my parents' condo, the sounds of the waves and the fishy smell of the salt air tease my mind. The shore draws me in. "Just give me a few minutes."

"Sure," they repeat in unison.

I am drawn to the surf. By the time I get to the water's edge, I've dropped my shorts, shirt, underwear, and bra. I stand, with just a towel covering me. I step on to the wet, shifting sand, feeling the splashing harmony of the cyclic waves. The late afternoon clouds cover the sun leaving the shore stripped of people.

Except for the rolling waves and squawking seagulls, the quiet swallows me. Everything is blue, light blue—the water, the sky, the air around me. Even the receding waves leave a mirror of blue upon the coquina sand. I drop the towel behind me. Slowly, I walk deeper into the blue water, feeling the warmth of it caress my feet, my calves, then knees, thighs, belly, chest, arms, neck, face, and finally my hair. While submerged, I empty my mind. I try to imagine God touching each part of my body, cleansing it to prepare me for my new life. I accept my beauty, my strength. I accept my direction as I search for wholeness with my creator. Rising from the waters, I recall special moments with Zack. I imagine those moments in terms of colors, textures, and scents. Goodness surrounds me as I submerge again. I float beneath the surface feeling the water's caress before I emerge back to the air, feeling lighter as my stress dissolves into the undertow.

My third emersion is my rebirth. I try to hold my breath longer as I feel so free and alive in this eerie, wonderful silence. Still submerged, I open my eyes. I see flashes of light in the blueness—the last rays of the sun descend beneath the dark clouds sending warmth to the waters that replenish me. I rise to the air with a gasp and a smile. A hint of peach and lavender begins to color the sky. My soul cries out in thankfulness for the beauty that surrounds me, for Zack, for my family, for my friends, for my ancestors, for the love that pours over me so abundantly.

I submerge one last time to celebrate my ocean mikvah. I am ready now for my life to begin anew with Zack. I swim against the incoming tide. When I rise I am beyond the breakers. I float in a bed made for me by Elizabeth, Ruth, Rebecca, Rachel, and Hannah. A bed made for me by Mama and Saphira, and by my grandmothers who died before I was born. For a fleeting moment, I feel as one with the God of Israel. My ancestors are smiling now. As I float I repeat a scripture I memorized as a child, "Surely, goodness and mercy shall follow me all the days of my life and I shall dwell in the house of the Lord forever".

These words touch me in a way I've never felt before. Turning over, I dive to the bottom. Never have I felt so free, so utterly accepted, so loved as I do in this holy paradise of blue. I swim along the sandy bottom and choke back the wrenching sobs that stir inside and are clamoring to be released with all this emotion and tension that's been building since my first dance with Zack. I know that when I walk down the aisle I will be new, even newer than I am at this precious moment.

I sit in the shallow water until I am surrounded by moonlight and then I make my way into the condo.

The only light is from candles and hurricane lamps strewn throughout the front room and out onto the deck. Katie and Beka embrace me. I try to explain this overwhelming emotion that has caught me so off guard—this phenomenon that fills my heart with absolute enchantment.

## 7

The dressing room off to the side of the synagogue is carpeted in rose pink. Bright sunlight shines from the only window, a huge skylight in the center of the ceiling. I stand, staring at my reflection in a tall three paneled floor mirror. "This is exquisite. If this gown doesn't make you famous, I don't know what will," I say while Beka laces up the corset back of my French satin gown.

Katie's screech causes the bustle of activity in this posh dressing room to come to a standstill. "Shelli. You're absolutely stunning." Katie stands next to me, looking as if she will wilt into tears. She stammers. "I've never seen you so, so, gorgeous."

"She's a bride. She's supposed to look gorgeous." Mrs. Levy waltzes toward me. "I am so fortunate," she says, as she takes my hands into hers, "that you love my only child—that today you will become a part of our family." Something passes between us—an understanding, an acceptance. I don't want to let go of her hand, so warm now. Such a contrast to the coolness of it in the past. I want so badly to say something about Emma, to let Mrs. Levy share her memories and her grief but instead, she asks me to call her *Mom*. We're bonded now. There will be a lifetime for listening and for sharing grief and joy.

"Don't make me cry, you guys." I swallow hard. "At least not until the reception."

Beka walks around me, looking at every detail, smoothing out the side pleat, straightening the train, nodding to herself.

"You're pleased, aren't you?" I look at her but she doesn't look back. Her attention is on my gown.

Mama stands behind Beka, cups her shoulders with both hands, and kisses her on the cheek. "We're so proud of you.

You studied hard. You made something beautiful of your life."

Beka's hands fly to cover her face.

"Let it go, sweetheart," Mama says. "Everything is so lovely because of you. Now, you cry a little then dry your tears and get yourself ready. It's almost time."

"The photographer's here," Saphira calls from the door. She suggests he begin with the flower girls and me while the rest of the bridesmaids help Beka, who's standing in the center of the room, barefoot in her dressing gown.

"Come, Naomi, Anna, have your picture taken with me." Naomi seems to drown in her little gown. She's lost more weight, even in the last few days since Beka made the final alterations. Mordie says she's in remission, that the tumor has shrunk. Until now, I believed him. The photographer has me sit on a cushioned stool and then arranges my nieces beside me. When Naomi gazes up at me with her sunken doe eyes, I pull her onto my lap. She squeezes my warm hand with her cold, frail one. Anna kneels, leans her head against my breast, and looks up at us. The photographer's flash catches the kiss I plant on Naomi's forehead. I immediately dismiss the thought that this day might be the last time I will see my sweet niece alive.

When Daddy comes in for the photo session, our eyes meet and there passes between us an unspoken sonnet of father-daughter delight. He holds me by the waist at arm's length. "Shayneleh," he says. I smile, understanding all that I am to him. Neither of us speaks more. My heart is full. I am no longer my father's little girl. My father is giving me to Zack, relinquishing his role of paternal responsibility as I become not only Zack's wife but a woman.

The photographer finishes and is off to the groom's room with Daddy and Zack's mother in tow. I imagine Zack, his groomsmen, and parents posing but the first click of the camera haunts my mind. Of all the wedding pictures, I fear that the first one will be the one I'll cherish above all the others.

"Anna, Naomi, are you ready?" I ask.

They join hands and grin. Their eyes glisten as much as their dresses shimmer.

"Aunt Shelli," Naomi says, looking up at me. Her eyes take in every inch from my translucent-white toenails, my silver, three-inch sandals, the beaded pleat of my gown and up to my veil covered face. "You're the most beautifulists bride I've ever seen."

"Most beautiful," Anna corrects, giggling.

I look at the two of them—one robust, one frail but both with angelic smiles. "You two are the most beautifulists flower girls I've ever seen." Naomi stares at me hauntingly, as if she knows something I don't know. I have to turn away.

When the music begins, I look at the way the bright colors of zinnias reflect off everyone's face and even off the swirls of the thousands of tiny glass beads that cover the bodice and peek from the pleat in my gown. I laugh at myself—such a zany idea of zinnias for a wedding but that's who I am. Everything is dreamy. I delight in my exquisite bouquet of family and friends.

Mama and Daddy hold tightly to my elbows as I look down at my bouquet. Daddy holds tighter as the petals of the zinnias begin to shake. Naomi leads the procession as Anna, Rachael, Katie, Beka, and Saphira follow. Zack and his parents walk arm-in-arm down the center aisle. They stop before the chuppah then turn to face me. Now, Mama and Daddy guide me to Zack and his parents. Zack kisses his mother, shakes his father's hand, and steps toward me. My heart pounds as our eyes hold each other's gaze. I see a tear run down the side of his nose. Zack lifts my veil, allowing my parents to kiss my cheeks. We share a spiritual moment as Zack reaches out to me, leads me to his side. Together we walk to our place under the chuppah. I'm glad that I don't see the faces of my parents following behind.

After the chanting of the Seven Blessings, I circle Zack seven times. With each circle, I feel this powerful, ancient gesture blessing us with Divine energy.

When we exchange our rings we repeat together, "I am my beloved's and my beloved is mine."

Zack and I repeat our vows, listen to the pronouncement, and drink from my parent's heirloom Kiddush cups—the same cups that they, my grandparents, great-grandparents, Saphira, Sol, Rachael, and Mordie drank from at their weddings. Suddenly, I feel dizzy from one swallow of wine on my fasting stomach. I cling to Zack for balance but feel more shaking in him.

All too soon, Sol recites the benediction. "May God bless you and keep you. May the light of God's presence shine upon you and be gracious to you. May God's countenance turn toward you, and grant you wholeness and peace."

The colorful ceramic cup, made lovingly for us by Zack's mother, is wrapped in a white cloth. It breaks as Zack stomps it. The congregation shouts, "Mazel tov."

I float down the aisle, my hand clinging to Zack's bulging bicep. We're ushered into a side room for our eighteen minutes of yihud, seclusion. A bottle of wine and two cups sit amongst a modest spread of kosher snacks on a white linen-covered table. This is our time to catch our breaths, break our fasts. A time to just be alone and savor the first few minutes of married life. Zack removes his yammica and prayer shawl then my headpiece and veil letting my hair fall to my shoulders. He pulls me to him and we kiss with the same passion we did almost ten years ago in the candlelit treehouse. I'm oblivious to Zack's zipper and his hands slipping my lace underwear to the side. All I feel is titillating excitement as Zack thrusts his desperate love into me without separating his warm lips from mine. It doesn't take long before we consummate our new status with joyful gasps and delight.

"I love you, Mrs. Zachary David Levy, I love you, Mrs. Shelli Segal-Levy. I love you, Shelli. I'll always love you."

I try to speak as a torrent of tears overtakes me. Joy tears. Love tears. Zack pulls me tighter to him. "If you don't want to talk," he says, "we still have fourteen more minutes of seclusion. We can do it again—slower this time." We laugh and hold each other's stare.


Zack's parents have arranged for an elegant white limousine to take us to the Siena Hotel on East Franklin Street. Tomorrow we will catch an early morning flight to Barbados. As I step into the elegance of the limo, I begin to relax after the frenzy of the past few days. I'm glad we had a Shabbaton before the wedding because, already, I can't remember much of the reception. The emotional upheaval intermingled with the joyous feasting and dancing seems like a dream already.

"I hope I spoke to everyone. Did you?" I say.

Zack just smiles, smoothes my hair.

"I'm sure we did," I say, as faces appear in my mind. "For the life of me, I can't recall one conversation. I can only remember dancing with Naomi."

"She stuck to you like glue—never let you out of her sight."

"I think we're attached at the hip. She looked better this evening, didn't she?"

Zack pats my hand.

We arrive at the hotel, a luxurious replica of an Italian Villa, and I feel as if we are far away when in reality we are less than two miles from home. Inside the lobby, we are met with a Tuscan elegance—Italian marble floors, majestic columns, European antiques, and a grand piano.

The bellhop escorts us to our room on the third floor. When he opens the door we are met with the aroma of roses and the same elegance as the lobby.

"It's so classy, isn't it?" I hold out my dress, twirl in a circle, while Zack pulls out his wallet facing the bellhop who is standing at attention in the middle of the room. I kick off my shoes and lean to inhale the biggest bouquet of long-stemmed red roses I've ever seen. "There must be five dozen." The bellhop closes the door behind him as I read the card, Welcome to our family, Shelli. We love you, Mom and Dad Levy. I turn to Zack. "Your parents have been so generous."

"They really like you, Shelli." Zack raises my head with his finger under my chin. "They love you like a daughter."

"I know. I hope I won't fail them."

"How could you?" Zack leans to kiss me with a passion that stirs my emotions.

"What's this?" Zack points to the coffee table where a box, wrapped up in sparkling translucent ribbons, awaits.

"It's from Beka and Katie. They told me to expect it."

Inside the box are two dozen round ivory candles, a box of matches, and two boxes of flat, mirrored candle holders. While I arrange the candles around the suite, Zack follows me with the matches then turns off the lamps.

"Now, come here," he says, holding his arms out to me. I float to him. His kiss ignites me causing me to feel like one of the candles—burning with desire, glowing, dancing in the breeze from the ceiling fan. "This gown is stunning and you look sensational but I like you better the way you were born."

Even though we've already consummated our blessed legal union with the quickie at our yihud, I am ravenous for Zack. His fingers sizzle against my skin as he unlaces the corset. His firm fingers slide to caress my hips and rise up my sides to my breasts. His breath is hot as he noses through my hair to plant a long, sensuous, kiss on the back of my neck. I go limp as my gown falls to the floor and I'm left in my Coco de Mer white lacy undies. This feeling is different. Married. I didn't think being married could deepen my affections or my emotions for this man I've loved for so long.

Zack slips my underwear down as he kneels before me, kissing me, belly button to toes. I touch the top of his head then bend slightly to remove his tie and see that his jacket is already on the floor. He eases me to the bed. I lay back watching him as he slowly unbuttons his shirt, removes his cufflinks, and sets them carefully on the dresser. He stands still in front of me, shirt unbuttoned, held open by his hands on his hips. I'm delighting in his striptease and am growing hotter by the moment. I know he knows it, that he is teasing me, tantalizing me. Now he lets the shirt fall to the ground, takes off his belt, unzips his pants, steps out of them and his briefs then his socks, one foot at a time. He stands before me, aroused, bronze, beautiful in the glow of the candles. If he stands before me any longer, I'm afraid I'll have a spontaneous orgasm. He smiles as if he hears my thoughts. I feel my body begin to shiver. My breathing turns to gasps. I reach out to him but he steps back, smiles, watches as my body performs a dance for him on its own. My eyes close, my back arches, I cry out in euphoria. Zack kneels over me still smiling as his tears drip onto my chest. Our honeymoon has begun.

## 8

Seven days of magic have passed in a bungalow perched high on a cliff in Barbados. The ocean view is as mesmerizing and enchanting as is our time together in this paradise. The bungalow came complete with a housekeeper who brings us hot fresh coconut bread every morning, turns on the coffee maker, stocks our shelves with fruit and snacks, and laughs when we don't have any dirty clothes for her to wash.

"This is our last day. Can you believe it? I want to stay here forever." I'm lying naked, stomach down, on a padded chaise lounge watching Zack gaze out at the ocean. His nude body is darker than ever. We haven't worn clothes for more than a couple of hours a day since we arrived here on the Platinum Coast.

Zack turns to me. "You're dazzling, Shelli. Just look at yourself—tan, robust, nipples standing at attention all day long." Zack runs a finger down the side of my face. "I've never been happier."

My heart melts. I set my rum cocktail on the floor. "Ravish me, you sun god," I say, as Zack laughs at his sudden erection.

"Little lover boy is loving this honeymoon," he says, as off we go to replenish our souls at the never empty well of blissful celebrations.

We've been home for four days, now, still living off the emotional high of our wedding and honeymoon. Zack is back to work while I'm busy writing thank you cards and trying to tie up loose ends before I return to school on Monday. When the phone rings, I welcome the interruption.

"Mama, hello." I can hear her crying. "Mama. What's wrong? What is it?"

Speaking between gasps she blurts out news I don't want to hear. "It's Naomi, darling."

"What about Naomi? What, Mama? Tell me."

"She's gone, Shelli. Mordie just called."

"No, Mama." I cry out. "No."

"She went to sleep, She never woke up. No pain, not for her, thanks be to God."

My mind goes back to the first wedding picture taken and the premonition I'd tried to ignore. An angry god has taken away the youngest of our brood. What have we done to deserve this? Naomi in her sweet innocence swept away like last night's garbage.

"What kind of a god can do this? What kind?" I cry into the phone.

I hear Mama take in a deep breath. "The funeral is tomorrow morning. We're leaving tonight on the first flight we can get. Will you come with us?" Mama's words swirl in my head. Of course I want to go tonight but I feel myself being torn, ripped down the middle. It's Thursday. Zack can't miss work tomorrow. He's just missed a week for our honeymoon. Yet, I need to be there with Mordie, Rachel, and especially Anna. I'm certain that Saphira and Sol and the boys will be there tonight too. Can I make this plan without Zack? If I wait a day for Zack and travel with him tomorrow night, we'll miss the funeral. Maybe I can go tonight, Zack can come tomorrow. I'm in a panic.

"Shelli, Shelli, are you there?" Now, Mama sounds as if she's in a panic.

"I'm here. I, I'll call you back. I need to call Zack." I have to calm down, get myself together.

"You call soon. Your father needs to make reservations."

"As soon as I can, Mama, as soon as I can."

Why do I feel so torn? Before the wedding, if something like this had happened, I'd have made an instant decision without feeling guilty. Where is this guilt coming from? Is this what marriage does to people? I have the phone in my hand but I can't make myself call Zack. I sit on the floor sobbing. The phone rings again and the vibration of it is like an electric shock. I drop it then fumble to pick it up again. "Hello."

"Shelli, I'm so sorry, sweetheart. Your dad just called. What do you want to do?"

Zack's voice immediately calms me. I try to stop my sobbing but can't.

"I know how much Naomi meant to you. Why don't you go with your parents this afternoon. I can catch a flight at six tomorrow morning."

I wipe my face with my arm, try to catch my breath. "What about work tomorrow?"

"I can work several hours this evening to make up for tomorrow. I've already checked with the boss."

"Oh Zack, you don't know what awful thoughts I was having. I love you so much." My tears are a torrent now—a torrent of anger, grief, worry, guilt even. How could I forget so quickly how perfect Zack is? I have to shake my head to gather my thoughts. "Breathe deep. Breathe deep again", I tell myself. "Okay, I'd like to go with my parents, as soon as possible."

"That's fine, honey. I'll be at Mordie's by eight."

"I love you, Zack."

"I love you too my beautiful princess. I love you too."


Tall trees shade Mordie's sprawling, old brick home from the yellow streetlights. Only a single candle from the front window illuminates this dark Baltimore night. Sol greets us without words. He leads us to where Mordie and Rachel are seated against the side wall. The furniture has been pushed back to line the walls. I try to ignore the small pine casket sitting alone in the center of the room, the focal point of the *living* room. There is no living here. Not tonight. I see the sad, tear-stained faces and question this ritualistic faith. This is the period of aninut, the time between death and burial when we're supposed to celebrate and appreciate life and be grateful for the life that was lived. We're supposed to reflect on that life, rather than mourn the death. Instead, we stare at the simple pine box. We see the shrouded shrunken still body. How can we celebrate life while sitting in this tomb? "Naomi." I cry out. I hear soft weeping behind me. I turn, fall to my knees beside my brother, Mordie. We cry as we hold one another tightly. This is the first time I've seen my brother cry. Feeling his tears, warm on my cheek, pulls me further into this terrible grief. Now, I feel Rachel's hand on my arm, squeezing. Her head presses against Mordie's and mine now. I feel her tears. Celebrate life, celebrate Naomi's life—that's what we're supposed to be doing now. I try to think of a way. Tomorrow, after the funeral, the grieving should begin. Not tonight.

Morning is breaking when I hear Zack's voice at the door. I feel the first note of this celebration song we're supposed to be singing.

He buries his head in my hair. I hold him so tightly I think I might break his ribs. "Did you get any sleep?" he asks as we separate slightly.

"We took turns napping but I couldn't sleep. I think I dozed off a couple times. While we were awake we sat by the casket, listening to Sol then the rabbi from Mordie's synagogue pray for Naomi's soul," I whisper. "It's ludicrous, isn't it? To pray that God will take Naomi to Gan Eden? To paradise? Isn't that a given? Why would God condemn an innocent child?"

Zack puts a finger to my lips as my voice grows louder. "Yes, it does seem redundant. Sounds like you need a little break. After I speak to everyone, will you take a walk with me?"

"Sure."

"There's a bakery just up the street that looks like it's about to open. We could get some breakfast rolls or bagels for everyone. There are also a couple of motels. We should get a room, right?"

"Right. Yes, a walk will do me good. Seeing you does me good."

Zack kisses my forehead and then begins his rounds consoling his new family. I step outside to sit on the porch steps. I don't want to hear anyone cry just now. I want to try somehow to celebrate this little girl's life. As the sun's rays begin to peek through the elm and maple trees that line the street, I sing a song to Naomi. I remember the first time I saw her. She was seven pounds, twelve ounces wrapped in the palest of pink ruffles. She was the last born of my nieces and nephews but she was the most beautiful. Suddenly she is alive, not dead. She giggles and dances, delighting my soul as I recall every moment I've spent with her. She blessed my wedding with her frail sweetness. She called me the most beautifulists bride—a gift I'll treasure forever.

"Ready?" Zack asks, interrupting my thoughts.

"Do they need something to eat?"

"Yes."

"Good. Can you get my bag? The funeral is at eleven. I really don't want to go back inside until after…"

"Sit tight. I'll be right back."


The sound of the ripping of Mordie's and Rachel's shirts by the rabbi during the funeral caused me to swallow back vomit. When someone began to wail, causing others to wail even louder, they  put a hand over my beautifulists Naomi's mouth and stopped her singing. Stopped her dancing. Made her die again. They buried her, alone in her pine asylum, under the shade of a great oak tree with no chance of being exhilarated by the sun or mesmerized by the moon. Alone. Lonely. Cold. Dark. For the life of me, I no longer see her as she lived. I only see her shrouded beneath mounds of dirt— shrouded with a hand over her mouth. My beautifulists Naomi.

Strapped into my seat on Southwest Airlines, heading to New Orleans for Katie's wedding, I feel pangs of disappointment. Zack has canceled out at the last minute. We've been planning Katie's wedding longer than our own. We've been looking forward to celebrating with her, Sean, and Beka in New Orleans. But his new boss sends him off to Prague, of all places, for a special meeting with technicians from all over Europe. The man in charge of the project, the one who was supposed to go, wrecked his car on I-40 and had a coronary because of it. Zack was the only candidate with the knowledge and information on the project to take his place. He claims he knows the project better than anyone. I can't believe he went so willingly, especially since we've had these plans for more than a year.

"The career ladder doesn't always come with easy choices," he'd said. "I have to accept assignments as opportunities…even if it means upsetting our plans."

We'd expected Zack to travel out of country for meetings sometime in the future but not so soon, not when I need him more than ever. My grief is raw for Naomi and all my family. *Why now?* I want to rid my mind of these sad thoughts.

I take in a deep breath. Pray for strength. Beka will meet my flight in a little less than two hours. Together we'll meet Katie and the rest of the female ensemble of her wedding party for afternoon coffee at Café du Monde. I inhale deeply and hold on to it for as long as I can. As I blow it out, I blow away this alien sadness. Katie will be radiant. In twenty-four hours she'll be walking down that wide aisle in Saint Louis Cathedral to the majestic tones of the huge pipe organ. I can't take this sadness with me. It's Katie's time for happiness. There's not a bone in my body that wants to take a shred of that happiness away from her big day. I have to be strong. I will be strong. I will be.

Two flight attendants, dressed in regulation white shirts, navy blue shorts, and white athletic shoes, push the refreshment cart slowly down the aisle selling drinks and snacks. When it stops at the row in front of me, the attendant at the rear of the cart nods to the man in the seat next to mine. "What would you like to drink?"

"Gin tonic, no ice."

She looks to me. I stare with my mouth half-open.

"Make that two," the man next to me says. "It's on me. You look as if you need a stiff one."

I glance at this man who is interrupting my thoughts, pushing his way into my life.

"Sorry," he says with a smile. "That wasn't a pick-up line."

"Thanks." I strain my voice to speak. "I'm not having a very good day."

"A good stiff drink will pull you up from the doldrums."

Doldrums. If he only knew.

The steward places napkins, empty plastic glasses, cans of tonic, and little green bottles of gin on our tray tables. "That will be five dollars each."

The man hands her some folded bills.

Like a shadow, I imitate this stranger. I remove the swizzle stick from the glass, place it on the napkin, pour an inch of tonic then the entire bottle of gin into my plastic glass. I remember taking a sip of gin when I was in college. I didn't like the taste. So, why am I drinking it now? I shrug, take a sip, then a gulp. I feel it burn. I swallow repeatedly until the glass is empty. The man next to me orders a second round, then a third.

Six days have passed since Naomi's funeral. All the family, except me, remains in Baltimore sitting Shiva, mourning for Naomi for the full seven days required. Aunts, cousins, grandparents aren't required to officially mourn but they're all there, together, holding each other up, praying the Kaddish, the prayer of mourning. I'm the only one to escape back into the world of the living. I couldn't miss the first week of the new term. I can't miss Katie's wedding. I am obligated. As if I'm the only one with a life that can't stop long enough to mourn my precious niece properly.

At the first meal after the funeral, we sat together eating hardboiled eggs and round unleavened bread to remind us that life is like a circle and that we who mourn have no words to describe our loss. There are no words, there never will be. Naomi is gone. No matter how much I believe in Olam Ha-Ba, the life after death where the righteous will be united with their ancestors, my heart feels the rotting stench of death. My brother, Mordie, my doctor brother who deals with death on a daily basis can't be comforted. The pain in his eyes, the way he wrings his handkerchief in his trembling hands, the way he tries, yet fails, to be strong stabs at my heart. I feel helpless to dry one tear. Children shouldn't die before their parents. Children shouldn't die. Death is for the old, not for a six-year-old, not for one so innocent, so pure, not for my beautifulists Naomi.

The words of the Kaddish are in the forefront of my mind. I close my eyes to hear them. Glorified and sanctified be God's great name throughout the world…He who creates peace in His celestial heights, may He create peace for us and for all Israel, and say, Amen.

I sip at the third gin repeating the prayer in my mind until I begin to feel comforted. As the attendant removes the trash from my table, I think about a favorite poem by Edna St. Vincet Millay. I change the words to suit my breaking heart, "More precious was the light in your eyes than all the zinnias in creation".

## 9

"Shelli, Beka. Over here." Katie calls from the far side of the Café du Monde on Decatur Street. As we make our way through the crowded canopied patio Katie meets us halfway then leads us to a long table with a festive view of Jackson Square, street artists, and a line of horse-drawn carriages. Katie's mother, stepmother, sister, stepsister, and three half-sisters simultaneously greet us. "Everyone, this is Shelli, my friend who just got married three weeks ago."

Before she can get to any more introductions, everyone is speaking—congratulating me, telling me they've seen pictures of my wedding that Katie and Sean took, telling me how special I am to Katie, how happy they are to meet me finally. On and on. Of course, I already know Katie's sister, Erin, and her mother, although it's been years since I've seen them.

"Wow. All my attendants are here at last." Katie presses her palms together in front of her mouth. Her ocean-green eyes sparkle.

Erin has grown into an attractive young woman who sports a diamond three times the size of mine. The other girls range in age from pre-teen to twenty and come in different shapes, sizes, and skin tones. Only one may be a little too busty and bottom-heavy to show off Beka's handiwork but teal is definitely going to work for all of us. I close my eyes to my sadness. I kiss Katie's cheek. "You're so beautiful today. I can't imagine how you're going to look tomorrow."

"Thanks for coming, Shelli. I know this is a bad time for you, especially with Zack being away, and...Naomi. I know how hard this is for you. Are you okay?"

"I'm fine. I wouldn't miss this for the world." I choke back the wail that fights within, kicking my stomach, lungs, and heart in an attempt to be set free.

A waiter brings us chicory-laced café au lait and the warm sugar-dusted beignets that Café du Monde is famous for. The half coffee, half chicory combo with scalded milk tastes good. It seems to perk up the numbness in my head left behind by the gin. We eat and chat before Katie gives each of us a pearl bracelet for a bridesmaid's gift before we break up into groups to see the sights or relax by the hotel pool before the rehearsal dinner later tonight. Beka chooses to nap at the hotel since she's exhausted after the last couple of days she's spent here putting the finishing touches on the gowns after the final fittings. Katie and I set off alone down Canal Street to see what we can find.

"Tell me all about your bachelorette party. I'm so sorry I couldn't be here." I try to keep the conversation focused on Katie.

"Since my stepsister and half-sisters aren't twenty-one it was rather tame for New Orleans. We ate at The Court of Two Sisters. It's an upper crust-tourist trap." Katie pauses, giving me a look I'm all too familiar with from childhood. "My mom chose it. I think she wanted to foot the bill at someplace expensive or maybe impressive, you know, just because she can afford it now and my father can't."

"I'm sure she wanted to make it nice for you, in addition to all the baggage."

"Well, she did that. The menu was fun—everything from escargot to Cajun dirty rice. Remember we were raised on Hamburger Helper." We both laugh. "But, wait 'till you hear this." She takes hold of my arm. "Later, the real party began. Beka and Erin took me to this club. It was weird at first, a bump and grind kind of place, past the Elysian Fields, over towards the Bywater district. The place looked a little seedy from the outside. It was packed and loud inside. Beka and Erin really got into the dancing. They sorta dragged me into it. It turned out to be fun. I've never seen Erin let her hair down, so to speak but she was drinking Bourbon shots as fast as she could get a guy to buy her one."

"Were you and Beka drinking Bourbon too?"

"Beka stuck with wine all night but I stopped after one glass of champagne. You know I got drunk once my first year at college. I learned my lesson. I didn't want a headache or a hangover to spoil the rest of the weekend." Katie shakes her head. "Everyone was dancing without partners. I wish you could have been there, Shelli. It's not something I'd want to do again but it was great for a bachelorette party. The last thing I wanted to see was a nude man jump out of a cake. This was kinky enough…raunchy even but lots of fun."

"I'm glad you enjoyed yourself. Sorry I wasn't there to share it with you."

"You did what you had to do. That's why I love you so much." Katie stands with her chin high. I can almost hear the thumping of her heart as well as the rumblings of her stomach.

The sun beats down on us as we walk. I begin to put Naomi and Zack into the back of my mind and focus on Katie's happiness. "Can you show me the real New Orleans, not the trendy, touristy side?"

"Do you want to see the area where I spent my last vacation?"

"If it's not too sad." Katie had volunteered with Habitat for Humanity to help build a house in the Lower Ninth Ward—an area still in shambles from the big hurricane in 2005.

"To be honest, it just might be sad. The progress has been so slow. I'd still like to take you there...to see how things are now."

"What do you mean?"

"Remember when I told you that the volunteers laid sod but didn't donate a lawnmower? Well, "I want to convince myself that the new owner has taken care of the house and the yard like she said she would."

We hail a cab and end up in the center of ramshackle homes with FEMA Xs marked on them. The absence of life is haunting. For every house still standing there are three or four platforms with driveways that go nowhere. Katie points in the direction she wants to go. The driver turns the car down an alley where half-naked children play on abandoned slabs and a couple of dark-skinned teenagers eye us with consternation. At the end is a bright blue pristine cottage with lace curtains blowing from the windows.

"That's it. That's the house I worked on. It's beautiful."

"And the lawn is mowed," I say.

When the driver stops the car, Katie asks him to wait. As we walk up the pansy-lined sidewalk the door swings open and a dark woman dressed in flowing, tie-dyed silk with an aqua turban shrieks before pulling Katie into an embrace. "When I sawed you come up the walk, I knewed it was my angel." She takes a step back. "Girl, you be mighty pretty today. Who with you? That Beka or Shelli?"

"Miss Betsy, this is Shelli." Katie speaks with a thrill in her voice and the proudest smile. She reaches for me. "Shelli, this is Miss Betsy DeLauro."

The woman wraps her generous arms around my neck, kisses one side of my face then the other. "I's so happy to meet a friend o' Miss Katie. Miss Katie 'bout saved my life."

Katie shakes her head. "It was a couple weeks' worth of painting that's all."

"Yes, ma'am. Paint and them listening ears. This girl done brought sunshine to Landry Street after so many years."

Miss Betsy pours her heart out to Katie while I listen. She appreciates the many volunteers but fears that too many years have passed, that the world has forgotten about the ubiquitous destruction of the Ninth Ward.

"So, is you married now?"

"Tomorrow, at Saint Louis Cathedral. Won't you come?"

"Naw. My spirits can't go disturbin' theirs. I just light a candle here for you. I light one for you too, Miss Shelli. I feel somethin' a stirrin' in you but you be okay." Miss Betsy shakes her head but doesn't smile. "Yes, ma'am, you be okay in a little while."

As we walk away, I ask, "What was that all about?"

"Black Magic, voodoo, I don't know for sure."

We look at each other and giggle but I feel frightened...as if Miss Betsy knows something or holds some power over me. I turn back. Miss Betsy is whirling and chanting on the front porch. I feel a chill just short of a convulsion.

We get back into the cab. Katie sighs. "Let's go to the Garden District, want to? There are some gorgeous Victorians there."

"You're the travel guide," I say, feeling relieved to be heading back into the trendy, touristy part of town. I wasn't as ready to get off the beaten path as I thought I was.

"I'm so glad to be with just you right now. You're giving me a chance to breathe. There's so much excitement and attitude with both my families together."

My frame of mind is off-kilter. I want to say something positive but I can't think of one word. I'm swinging between anger, sadness, happiness, saneness, insanity. Right now, I just want to sit down and bawl my eyes out. I certainly have reason to have mixed feelings. I take in a deep breath, try to keep from sinking. There's no happiness in my life that I can instantly recall. I feel like a lost child. Abandoned. Alone. The pain is suddenly more than I can bear.


At the rehearsal dinner, I meet a shirttail cousin of Katie's, Gregoire Sebastian, an assertive New Orleanian with piercing gray-blue eyes and an irresistible, soft, Cajun-southern gentleman inflection in his voice. That is until he puts on this Irish brogue, I think to impress me.

"Ya don't look Irish, do ya?" He looks at me through dark blond hair that hangs over one eye. As he brushes it away, I notice manicured, buffed nails.

"No, laddy, there's no a bit o' Irish here."

"Well, what the hell is a gorgeous dame like you doing in a place like this without your husband?" Now, he sounds like Humphrey Bogart in *Casablanca*.

I glance at my wedding ring.

"Sorry, did I say somethin' wrong?" Gregoire leans toward me, looking deep into my eyes.

"It's a long story."

"I do have all weekend, Madam."

"Can you get me out of here? I don't drink beer and I don't know one word of these Irish drinking songs."

"Me neither. It's not my style. But I do know the perfect place."

Perfect place? What could this person know of perfect places? Zack and I have so many perfect places. I can't let myself think about Zack right now. I have to get through twenty-four more hours. Just twenty-four. Then I can let go. In twenty-four hours I'll be home in Zack's arms, in our warm bed. I feel the corners of my mouth curl. "You're on."

Gregoire takes me by the arm.

"Wait, I need to tell Beka I'm leaving."

"Tell her she can come with, if she wants."

Beka declines coming along but accepts a ride back to the hotel. Tomorrow will be a big day for her too making certain all the gowns are to perfection.

"What do you drink?" Gregoire asks, as we drive toward the French Quarter in his silver Lexus IS 350 with the top down.

The word, gin, slips through my lips like it's at the top of my vocabulary.

"I told you, *cher*, I know the perfect spot."

"Am I dressed for it?" I look at my casual sundress. Gregoire looks like a thin, young Colonel Sanders in his cream-colored suit.

"You're sensational in hot pink."

"It's watermelon."

"Excuse me, m'dear. You're sensational in watermelon."
He touches the thin cotton that covers my thigh.

When we arrive at Lafitte's Blacksmith Shop, Gregoire informs me that this is one of the finest bars in New Orleans and one of the few remaining original French architecture structures in the French Quarter. He leads me to a table on the patio, next to a sculpture of Adam and Eve embracing on a bed of ivy then tells me the history of the sculpture, the bar, and another bar down the street called Lafitte's Exile. He orders two Obituary cocktails—a gin martini with half a jigger of Pernod. The Pernod, he says, is licorice liquor, a relative of ouzo. He talks while I drink. He seems to know just about everything there is to know about New Orleans or at least he's convincing me he does. He offers to take me back to his place but I decline. I just need to hold myself together. I tell him that this one drink will do.

My head's in a fog when he drops me off safely at the hotel. Beka is asleep, so I tiptoe to the shower, stand under the hot water until I feel as if I'm going to pass out, and then drop into bed without drying off. I'm almost home free.

An early morning drizzle with thick hanging fog gives way at noon to bright blue skies and sunshine hot enough to bake crayfish and grits on the sidewalks. White flower-bedecked horse-drawn carriages wouldn't have been much fun in the rain for a bride and her court on a July afternoon. Katie is more than radiant. She's angelic, flawless, ethereal. Her curly ginger hair bounces on her shoulders around her unblemished skin and her great big pure heart. I smile as I'm caught up in her happiness.

Beka stands back. She's not smiling but has a look of satisfaction and pride even though no one has complimented her yet today on her gift. Feeling almost as beautiful as I did at my own wedding, I go to her and take her hands in mine. "You did it, Beka. This wedding will get you noticed. Look at everyone. Just look. I'm so proud of you."

"Thanks, Shelli." Beka touches my arm. "Something's troubling you, isn't it? I mean, I don't know what I mean. There's just this look in your eyes. Something's not right."

I take in a deep breath. I push Zack and Naomi away. "I'm fine. I just need to scream." I look to the floor. "I need to scream but nothing comes out." I shake my head to keep the tears from erupting. "This day is Katie's, not mine. I can't…"

"Oh Shell. Damn." she says, squeezing my hands harder, standing straight, biting her bottom lip. "What can I do?"

"Pray that I make it through the wedding."

"The carriages are waiting." Katie calls from across the room.

Away we go, attendants first, followed by our own Cinderella.

## 10

My palms are beginning to bleed from pushing my fingernails into them, trying to hold myself together. The long, dreary Latin Mass during the wedding taunts my nerves giving me too much time to dwell on my problems. My anger at Zack and God seethes in this building of crystal chandeliers, painted ceilings, and ridiculously sad-looking icons. Are they sad because their god has raped this world and murdered its children?

Finally, the reception begins at the grand Le Pavillon Hotel, my last hurdle. Gregoire sees my distress, rescues me with one inviting outstretched hand and a gin tonic in the other. I can make it, now. I know I can.

We sit at one of the decorated tables. I lift the glass to my lips. The gin feels like ice in a hot, dusty desert as it passes through my parched throat. I drink it quickly, then ask for another. Soon I'm drinking gin on the rocks. The tonic nauseates me but the gin slips down my throat igniting a fire inside. Gregoire keeps my glass full. I feel as if he's protecting me. I look at him and smile. He plants a deep, long, wet kiss on my mouth. When I come up for air, I meet with Beka's strange stare.

"Shelli. Let's go to our hotel."

"Why? I don't want to miss all the fun."

"I think you've had too much to drink." Beka has tears in her eyes. "You're going to regret this tomorrow. Come on, Shell. Katie and Sean have left. The party is breaking up. Come with me. Please."

There's a full martini glass in front of me. I drink it down in three swallows. "This is what I need right now. I need to drown this whole god dammed world out." The sound of fury in my voice frightens me. "I don't need to be nursed." My burning desire for the taste of flesh is compulsive. As if Gregoire has read my mind he guides my hand to his erection under the tablecloth then leans back, groans in pleasure. Lust grips me. Beka yells for us to leave. Gregoire suggests a game of truth or dare. He dares Beka and me to flash our breasts New Orleans style so I do. Beka is literally screaming at me while Gregoire laughs. I watch them as if I'm in a dream or a fog. I wave Beka away. Next thing I know the manager is escorting Gregoire and me out the front door with Beka on our heels.

"Shelli. Stop. Come with me. Please, Shelli. Please don't go with that maniac. Please."

"Did you see the scowl?" I look at Gregoire's amusing half-smile. "I've never seen Beka so angry. I didn't think she had it in her."

"Your friend, as you call her, needs some tamin' and do I know the people who could do the job." Gregoire steadies me as we descend the front steps to the sidewalk. The hotel manager stands in the open doorway telling us not to come back or he'll call the police.

"Call the police, you mother fucker." Gregoire shouts as the door slams behind us. "The Chief of Police just happens to be one of my finest clients."

"Are you a lawyer?" I ask.

"Me? No, I am not but thank you for the compliment. You are one fine lady." Gregoire looks up the street. "What's your fancy?"

"I'd like to get out of this dress." I kick off my shoes, sending them tumbling down the sidewalk.

"Let me, darlin'—you just might need these later." Gregoire retrieves my shoes, sticking one in each jacket side pocket. "Come on, now. I know just the place."

"You seem to know plenty of right or perfect places, don't you?"

"That's my job."

"What is?"

"What is what?"

"Sorry, what's your job? What do you do for a living?"

"I entertain for a living, I *live* for a living." Gregoire puts his arm around my waist pulling me to him. It isn't the same as when Zack does it. This is stronger, sexier, almost wicked.

"You're in show business?"

"I started out as a tour guide. I've done it all in Nawlins. History tours, old home tours, riverboat tours, cemetery, and ghost tours. I can show you where Billie Holliday first sang as well as the Creole Songbird, Esther Bigeou. Why, I even know just about everthing 'bout Nawlings even where Satchmo and cocktails were born. You name it, I know 'bout it. Then one fine day, and I do mean fine, I meet this gentleman who offers me a position as his personal entertainment manager." Gregoire stops, looks at me. "You don't have a clue what I'm saying, do you?"

"Just because I can't walk a straight line doesn't mean I don't comprehend. I am lucid."

"That's what I like about you. You're not a cheap date."

"Cheap?"

"Inexpensive. I mean you can drink the pants off a sailor and still be lucid. A rich man would soon be poor if he had to supply your liquor."

"So, what does a personal entertainment manager do?"

"Anything the man wants. He asks, I deliver."

"Deliver what?"

"Everthing—grand parties, trips, booze, women, men even."

"For his company?"

"No, for him, personally. Sometimes for a few very intimate, anonymous friends."

"Oh. What does he do for a living?"

"Inherited an extremely legitimate and lucrative business that just 'bout runs itself. He's a billionaire, I would imagine. Just works an hour or so a day, so he has lots of time to play."

"What's the company?"

"That's all I can say 'bout him. I'm not at liberty to divulge the details."

"You're not doing anything illegal are you? Is he?"

"No. Everthing's above board. Consentin' adults." Gregoire reaches into his pocket to pull out a set of keys, unlocks an iron gate, and holds it open for me. "After you, Madam."

We step off Orleans Avenue into a hidden garden complete with a mosaic tile, lighted fountain. "You live here?"

"On the second floor, with a view of the city lights, if you please. Come, the stairs are just to the left."

Inside, the apartment looks like an eclectic Mardi gras museum has merged with the Historical Society of New Orleans. I have to look close to see that the walls are purple. There's barely a space without a photograph, painting, or poster depicting New Orleans in its beauty, excitement, and celebrations as well as its dark corners of degradation and debauchery. The furnishings are lavish. Nothing appears to be a hand-me-down unless it's from some wealthy person's estate sale.

From behind, Gregoire slowly unfastens my gown. He pushes his body hard against my back. I feel his erection throbbing. He wraps his arms around me and takes one breast in each hand as he sucks hard on the side of my neck until I can feel the blood clot there. I know I'll have a souvenir to take home. "I just happen to have some very special gin, mon cher," Gregoire says after releasing his lips from my neck. "Would you like some?"

"Of course, on the rocks." I step out of my gown, leaving it crumpled on the floor.

"Oh my precious one, this gin doesn't need rocks." Gregoire hesitates, stares at me.

I realize that I am standing before him, comfortably, in just my lacy underwear. When I smile and cover my breasts with my hands, he steps into the kitchen. I survey the room until he returns with two strange glasses.

"Your special gin?" I take a sip. "It's good," I say feeling an uncanny arousal.

"It's TEN by Tanqueray. This is, to be sure, the ultimate martini. No ice in the glass to water it down, not an olive or even a hint of lime zest, and definitely no vermouth. I store the glasses in the freezer."

I hold the glass at eye level. It's actually two glasses in one, a martini glass without a stem sits in a goblet of crushed ice so the syrupy liquor, which has more legs than a thick red wine, doesn't get diluted. "It's better than gin. It's the best gin I've tasted but the glass, it's quite unique. What ostentatious ideas you do have, sir. You're so upscale, you know?"

"What do you mean?"

"Drinking trendy gin from trendy, frozen glasses."

"Just like you…" Gregoire takes my hand. "Let's get rid of those darlin' little pantaloons. Come, the bedroom waits."

I sit on an upholstered stool in front of an ornate rosewood vanity. Gregoire sets his drink on the nightstand and turns to me as he disrobes proudly. I try to look away but I stare at him as if he is a king or hero I long to worship. He takes my gin and places it next to his on the nightstand. "Am I rushing you?"

"No." I laugh. "I'm in awe."

"You are my breath of fresh air." He reaches out to me. "I need a woman like you."

I hesitate, before slowly removing the underwear I wore at my wedding. *This is for you, Zack*, I think as I toss them over my shoulder. I literally fall into Gregoire's arms.

His kiss is hot, frantic, as if he's waited as long as he can to take pleasure in me. He backs me into the wall, grabs my thighs, as I wrap my legs around him. After three or four thrusts he comes with force so strong that I can feel the explosion in the pit of my stomach. He groans then quickly lowers me to the bed.

"Hey. What about me?" I am voracious. My desire is desperate, overpowering, unbearable.

He lifts his glass, takes a long swallow before returning the glass to the nightstand. "Spread your legs, my beauty," he says as he ducks his head and takes me to a place I've never even dreamed of—a place I didn't know exists. I squirm in pleasure but it doesn't begin to fulfill me. "More. More." I shout.

The passion, sweat, and gin continues for hours until Gregoire passes out, face down with an arm draped across my belly. I'm still ravenous even though I've had orgasm after orgasm. I shake his limp body while I plead to be satisfied but he doesn't wake up. The sun is up now and I notice dust on the purple walls. I close my eyes and sleep. I dream of myself on my wedding day walking down the aisle in a shroud and a purple-feathered mask.

I awaken with a jerk. I have an ungodly headache. Gregoire's still passed out so I recover my clothing and head out to find coffee. I'm getting used to the stench of the French Quarter—it seems like home to me.

When I open the hotel room door, I find Beka sitting at the foot of the bed with her phone on her lap, looking like a sick puppy.

"Shelli, what's going on? Where did you go last night? Why didn't you answer my calls?"

"First I turned my cell off since you wouldn't stop calling then I went to Gregoire's for a nightcap." I smirk. "Everything's fine. I just needed to sleep off the booze. I don't think I'll ever go to an Irish wedding again." I kick off my shoes. "I brought you a coffee and some pastries."

"Thanks," she says. I see that familiar scowl as she reaches for the bag but has her eyes on the crumpled gown. "I was so worried, Shell. What happened at the reception? What was that scene all about?"

"Get off it, Beka." I'm feeling agitated now. "It was nothing. I was just trying to forget Zack and Naomi. I was trying to have a little fun."

"You call allowing a deranged stranger to mall you in public fun?"

"He had a little too much to drink, that's all. It was innocent fun. What kind of person do you think I am?"

"Until yesterday I thought you were the predictable friend you've been for twenty-five years. I've never seen you act this way. Just look at yourself…"

"What?"

"Look at your neck. I've never seen you with a hickey." Beka wipes tears from her face with a corner of the bed sheet.

"Don't get upset with me. It was you who put the idea of outrageous sex into my mind in the first place."

"What are you talking about? You're married, Shelli, or did you forget that?"

"A hickey isn't going to ruin what I have with Zack." I go into the bathroom, splash cold water on my face. Beka's tears irritate me to hell.

"Did you run off with this Casanova to get back at Zack for being sent to Prague?" Beka follows me, stands at the bathroom door. "Is this your way of dealing with anger? Look at me, Shelli. Are you trying to put a crack in your perfect world?"

"I'll meet you back here at noon," I say, as I slip into a pair of khaki shorts and a white camisole. "I can't take anymore interrogating."

"Aren't you forgetting something?"

"Like what?"

"Like a shirt?

"What in the hell do you call this?" I ask as I pull at my strap.

"I call that underwear, especially without a bra."

"Well, it's hot outside and this *is* Nawlins."

My arousal heightens as I walk out into the mid-morning sun. I'm as sure-footed as a donkey on a cliff but my head is a foggy seashore. My nipples are hard. I resist the temptation to touch them. I walk in the shade looking for someone to extinguish the fire that is burning out of control. I sit on a bench in the shade of a leafy oak near Jackson Square afraid I'll faint from the heat and my overpowering lust. A man walks by, I smile when he stops. We chitchat until I've seduced him. He suggests a historic bar around the corner and a cool drink. I accept.

The bar is dark inside. As soon as we order drinks we get it on quickly against the wall in the men's bathroom. He frantically pounds into me and it's over way before I'm ready. I'm left aching, agonizing for more but he's apparently satisfied. He leaves me with my shorts and underwear around my ankles. I pull them up, hammer my fists against the wall. My insides are in a spasm as I walk out of the restroom completely unsatisfied. I return to stand behind the man, who is nursing a beer at the bar. I suppress my anger as I gulp my gin. I rub my breasts against his back until he is aroused again. The bartender sets a second round in front of us. I guzzle the martini to quench this craving, to be satisfied, satiated, set free. The man swivels around on the barstool to face me, slips his hands under my camisole. Before long we're banging away in the bathroom again. Banging our way to more emptiness than I've ever known. He leaves me without a word.

I stop at a Starbuck's on my way to the hotel and order a triple espresso to clear the fog before heading back to the hotel to pack for my trip home.

As expected, Beka is waiting for me. She's packed, dressed, and sitting on the edge of the bed. "Good. You're back in time." She looks at me blankly. "I took the liberty to pack most of your things."

"Thanks," I say. I walk to the shower, let scalding water wash over me again but it doesn't take away the ungodly desires of my flesh. I don't want to leave the shower. I don't want to leave New Orleans. When I feel as if I'll faint, I turn the water off and step out of the shower. Beka folds a towel and her arms around me. I feel nothing.

On my flight home, I order two miniatures of Tanqueray and guzzle it straight from the bottles. I'm in a panic. I want to run to the door and jump out—jump out into freedom. I grasp the armrests with all my might.

The apartment in Chapel Hill is too quiet. My phone rings but I don't answer. I just listen to the voice mail. "Shelli, sweetheart, I'm afraid I have more bad news. The presentation had some holes in it, so the meeting ran over. Now, I'm on my way to London to see if I can work out some kinks there. I'm afraid I won't be home until the end of next week. Call me, please. I need to hear your voice. I love you, Shelli."

"Damn. Damn. Damn. London, my ass. There's another woman. I knew this would happen. Damn the son of a bitch." I plop onto the sofa. "What the fuck am I going to do now?" I look at the stack of thank-you notes that need to be addressed and mailed. "Fuck that." I pick them up, carry them to the kitchen sink and burn them, one by one. Then I drive down to the nearest ABC store and buy a liter of Tanqueray.

My phone won't quit. First Beka, then Mama, then Beka, and Mama again the whole livelong day. I don't answer. I just wait for Gregoire.

Just before sunset, Mama lets herself in. I meet her with a glass of gin in one hand and a cigarette in the other. She stands in the foyer. "Shelli, why didn't you answer the phone or call me?"

"Come in," I say but she hesitates, looking at me as if I am some kind of freak. "Come in. I don't bite."

"What is it? Something's wrong."

I take a long drag off the cigarette and blow the smoke straight up as I flick the ashes into an empty coffee cup.

"Why are you smoking? You don't smoke, Shelli."

"Well, I do now. I just started today." I light up another. "Smoking relieves my nerves."

"Your nerves—are on edge."

"You can say that again." I inhale until my lungs burn then blow blue-gray smoke into the air slowly and defiantly, watching as it streams straight up and mushrooms like the aftermath of the atomic bomb.

"Tell me, Shelli. What's bothering you?" Mama sits on the sofa.

I pace in front of her. "Everything is bothering me. Everything."

"Like what, princess?"

"First I marry a worthless womanizer who's making it with every woman in Europe, then Naomi ups and dies. On top of all that shit, Beka accuses me of adultery. Of course, I committed adultery. It was the only way to get back at that cheating bastard of a husband. Fuck him. Fuck the world."

"Shelli." Mama contorts her face as if she's looking at a two-headed, one-eyed baby on the cover of a tabloid. "Zack loves you. Why are you saying such awful things about him? About Naomi."

"Let's not talk about her—she's dead. And so should Zack be."

"I come here to comfort my daughter but my daughter is not here. You are not my Shelli. You are *not* my Shelli."

"Then you are not my mother, so just fuck off."

"I'm calling your father. I don't know who you are but you are not...my...Shelli." My pathetic mother turns her back and leaves, just like my pathetic husband and my pathetic niece. What the hell is wrong with everybody?

Another call comes in, I wait for my voice mail while I bang the phone on the kitchen counter. I listen to my advisor at Duke asking where I am. Shit. I'm in hell. Why won't everyone leave me alone? I pour the last of the gin into a flask, grab my bag, and catch the next flight to New Orleans before my father shows up.

"Mon cher, welcome back." Gregoire holds me in his arms. For the first time since I left him, I feel completely safe. "You're shakin'." He holds my face in his hands. "I know how to fix that. A specialty, or maybe three, that you haven't witnessed yet. Why don't you get out of those hot jeans? There's a silk robe hanging on the dressin' room door. I need to make a couple of calls."

I strip, leaving my clothes in a heap on the floor. The shower looks enticing so I step in. I let the scalding water soak my hair. I see a perfumed shampoo so I douse my head.

"First aid," Gregoire says as he pulls back the shower curtain. He has disrobed—his erection reaches for the sky.

I lean against the warm tile and enjoy his thrusting from behind. I'm turned on by the pleasure sounds he's making but it's over too soon. "That was nice but I need more than a quickie."

"There's more where that came from, cher. Much more. You just got a little appetizer."

"Really?"

"Sit at the vanity," he instructs. He exchanges my towel for a glass of gin and begins to dry my hair.

I feel calm now like I'm in a safe haven. I watch Gregoire in the mirror. He puts the towel down and massages my knotted neck. "My, my. I like this attention to detail."

"Just wait. The best is soon to come."

"What's that?" I ask, relaxing now.

"Reinforcements, Madam. You're much too hot to handle alone."

"Really? Tell me more."

"I've never met a woman so voracious. I've never met a woman I couldn't satisfy."

"But you got me so close."

"Ah, the doorbell rings. I need to exit stage left. You can put on that robe or meet them in the buff…like me."

I put on the silk robe before combing my hair. The inextinguishable burning of my groin is insufferable. Gregoire has just made things worse for me. Now I have to face people I don't know. My mind races as I try to find an excuse to get Gregoire into bed and get rid of the dammed company. I sip the gin, feeling it burn all the way to my stomach.

"Come on in, my darlings. Your drinks await on the bar." I hear Gregoire conversing with a male and a female. I let them be while I add a little blush to my cheeks from a basket of cosmetics on the mahogany vanity.

"Shelli, come meet the Second Guard," Gregoire calls.

I reluctantly stand and sidle towards Gregoire's voice. "Hello," I say as I walk into the living room.

"Hi, Shelli, I'm Rosalie." The young woman blinks thick, black lashes like a fan. She reaches out to shake hands. Turning but still holding my hand she says, "This is our dear friend, Jonathan."

I assume Jonathan is Gregoire's patron, although he appears younger than I'd imagined. He's dressed in a steel blue Luciano Carreli suit that brings out a rosy glow in his almost black skin. We stare into each other's eyes while he slowly reaches out to gently take my hand from Rosalie's.

"Shelli, it is a pleasure to meet you." His accent is thick Creole-French which enchants me. His warm handshake and deep gaze relax yet excite me until I have to look away. "It looks like I'm a little overdressed for the occasion. Do you mind…?" He loosens his silk tie, hands it to Gregoire then begins to unbutton his shirt, revealing his dark shiny hairless chest.

"Go right ahead." I gasp, feeling a tingle where his hand held mine.

"Show her, Jonathan. Show her what she wants to see."
Gregoire nudges him in the ribs. "She's heard all the stories
of how much bigger and longer Negroes are."

Jonathan laughs, runs a hand over the bulge in his pants.
"Yeah, you're the first white man that can hold a candle to
me." Jonathan removes his jacket, unbuttons his shirt, and
begins to unfasten his belt. I look away.

"Ignore them, Shelli," Rosalie says, pulling me to the
sofa to sit next to her. "Gregoire, refills, if you will." Rosalie
takes the glass from my hand, hands it to Gregoire before she
slips off her shoes. "Gregoire says you're from North
Carolina."

"That's right. Chapel Hill." I sit up straight, push my
bottom hard into the sofa. My level of arousal is off the scale.

"So, how did you meet? Were you here on vacation?"

"No, a wedding. I was a bridesmaid in one of those
ridiculous dresses. Gregoire is a cousin of the bride. He
actually rescued me from an Irish drinking party the night
before the wedding."

"And took you to Lafitte's. Don't forget that part, love."
Gregoire winks over his shoulder.

"Ah, Lafitte's." Rosalie sighs loudly. "Isn't that where
you took me on our first date?"

"I take everyone there, even Jonathan."

Rosalie stands to pull her shirt over her head. She
unfastens her denim shorts, letting them fall to the ground
leaving her glistening, sweaty body completely nude. "It's
too hot in here for me."

My chin drops. I take in a little gasp. When she bends
forward I inhale the scent of lilacs. She twists her waist-
length sandy blond hair into a tight figure eight bun then
secures it with a chopstick from a jar on the coffee table.

Her body excites me. I'm astounded by the fact. She's
shorter, smaller than me with barely visible fine blond hair
on her arms and legs. Her breasts are beautiful—so large that
they sag on her otherwise tight body. I long to touch them but

restrain. I clench my fists until I feel my fingernails penetrate my already scarred palms.

Gregoire stands behind Rosalie as she bends at the hips, letting her breasts sway in front me. "Relax." She looks me straight in the eye. "You don't have to do anything you don't want to. We're friends here, friends who happen to enjoy sex. You're welcome to join us or just watch. Ohh, ahh, Gregoire." She turns her head to look back at him. My breath catches. I've never seen another couple engaged in sex. I'm mesmerized watching Gregoire's thrusting and grinding and listening to Rosalie's joyful moaning. My face must show surprise or awe.

"We're consenting adults." Jonathan raises his glass as if to toast my initiation. "Gregoire thinks you'll enjoy our fun."

I can't take my eyes off Rosalie and Gregoire as they sway in rhythm while Gregoire continues his pleasure.

Jonathan clears his throat. His smile tells me he's enjoying my voyeurism. He walks toward me. When he's a breath away he tugs gently the sash of my robe. "Why don't you slip out of this," he says.

Without taking my eyes off his I let the silk robe fall to the floor.

"May I?" Jonathan traces the outside curve of my breast with one finger. He lets his slacks slip to the floor.

"Of course." His large, warm hands cover my breasts. I throw my head back and gasp. I want to be ravished.

While Jonathan caresses me, tears of relief brim my eyes. The excitement is overwhelming.

"Come, my darlings," Gregoire says as he leads the way to the bedroom.

I feel a nudge as Jonathan presses against my back. Gregoire throws back the comforter on the California king bed to reveal violet satin sheets. Before I can catch my breath, I'm on my back. Jonathan is inside me, filling me up while I drown in Rosalie's breasts as she kneels over me. I feel Gregoire's hand stroke my breasts as he leans over

Rosalie and rocks in rhythm with her until she screams out in pleasure. I am consumed by warm hands, mouths, tongues. My head spins. I feel blood pumping through my jugulars. The taste of salt on tight skin mingles with whiffs of sweat, cologne, and musk. A hard kiss presses against my teeth. Someone calls out to Jesus. Suddenly Jonathan pulls out and I'm flipped onto my hands and knees like a ragdoll. I'm entered from behind while my body, every inch of it, is massaged, pinched, sucked, coddled. I'm drowning in nirvana. I scream out in pleasure and pain and beg for more. Rosalie moans in delight. She's stretched out facing me, smiling. Her eyes, the approval in them, tug at something deep inside me. She rolls toward me, takes one of my breasts into her mouth, sucks it deep into the back of her throat. My nipple tingles to a point of pain that excites me like nothing ever has. I feel a tightening in the hollow of my pelvis—the release of some strange satisfaction, some new sensation of mind over body. I'm flipped to my back again and watch as Jonathan thrusts into me while calling Gregoire to fuck him before it's too late.

My burning is out of control as I'm swept into this surreal world of Nawlins.

## 11

"What did you expect me to do, Zack?" I yell from our bedroom. "You spend two fucking weeks in Europe and expect me to sit home while you fuck everything in lacy underwear."

"Stop saying that, Shelli," Zack says. "Please. What's gotten into you?"

"Stop saying what?"

"Fuck. You've never used that word."

"Well, it's a big part of my vocabulary now, especially since fucking women behind my back is something you've kept hidden from me all these years. Why didn't you have the guts to tell me about it before we got married? I would never have married a cheat like you."

"Shelli, calm down." Zack reaches out for me but I pull away. "I'm not a cheat. I promised you that I'd never cheat and I never have. Why don't you believe me?"

"Because you're a fucking liar, that's why."

"Look, Shelli, it's like this. Your parents are worried sick, so are mine, so is Beka. Thank God you haven't gotten to Katie yet."

"I will, if she takes up sides with all of you."

"No one's taking sides. We all love you. You're out of control. You're drinking a bottle of gin a day. That's not normal. It's not you. Can we just sit down and have a civilized conversation?"

"Civilized? I'm the only one here who's civilized. Everyone else has gone fucking mad. Will you just all leave me alone? God. I need air. I need freedom. Why can't you apologize to me for wrecking everything?"

"Excuse me. I'm not wrecking anything—you are. Please let me take you to see your parents. Something's wrong, Shelli. Something's very wrong. We need help to figure it out. Please—"

"No, you shut up. You make me sick." I grab my keys on my way out the door. "I'll see you later, if you're lucky." I climb into my car. As if on autopilot, the car heads straight for the airport.

I knock on Gregoire's door. Rosalie answers. "Oh honey. It doesn't look as if things went well at home. Come on in. I have just what you need. Gregoire is out on business. He asked if I'd take care of you."

"Everyone's been a bitch at home. I don't know what I did to deserve all their hate. They're people I don't know anymore. I don't care to know. I want to be with you and Gregoire. I want to stay here in New Orleans."

"Good." She takes hold of my hand. "You're shaking. Let me fix you a drink. Gin okay?"

"Yeah. Is it alright if I stretch out on Gregoire's bed?"

"Of course. I'll give you a massage if you want. Sounds like you need one."

"That'd be great." I undress in front of the vanity mirror. My body is hard and fit. Ripe. I need to be relieved of this overwhelming sexual tension. I can't stop staring at my nudity.

"You're lovely." Rosalie hands me the gin. "You don't need to stare at yourself to confirm it."

"Sorry, it's just since I met Gregoire, I can't, well, I can't get enough sex." I down half the gin in two swallows. "Does sex satisfy you?"

"Usually. Why?"

"I mean, can you go for a few hours without thinking about it, without wanting it?"

"Sit on the side of the bed, let me massage your shoulders." Rosalie pushes me gently, removes her clothes, and then climbs in bed behind me. "What are you getting at?"

"I'm horny all the time, like a nymphomaniac. Nothing satisfies me."

"Nothing?"

"Well, I'm satisfied for a while but never totally. I don't know. It's like the more I get, the more I want. The more I get, the emptier I feel."

"Maybe we should try some toys."

"Toys?"

"Gregoire has a closet full of costumes, vibrators, leather whips, chains, stuff like that."

"Will he show me how it all works?"

"Probably. He doesn't like it much, I mean S&M, but he keeps it for his boss and his boss' associates."

"Is Jonathan Gregoire's boss?"

"Perhaps. But Gregoire doesn't admit it."

"Who else would his boss be? You?"

Rosalie laughs. "Heaven's no. I'm a well-paid prostitute. I have a contract not to mess around with anyone but Jonathan, Gregoire, or anyone they bring here."

"So you fool around with me because they pay you?"

Rosalie moves to sit next to me. She kisses my mouth while she walks two fingers sensuously up my thigh. "I have to admit that I get paid very well to give you what you need."

"Why?"

"Because Gregoire and Jonathan want to keep you around."

"Oh."

"Jonathan likes it when women play together. My job is pleasing you and them—not getting involved personally. But you know what?"

"What?"

"I do feel a fondness for you. I enjoy making you feel good. Besides, it's nice having another female around."

Thanks," I say, lying back, propping my head on a pile of down pillows. "I've never been physically involved with a woman...I, um, never wanted female attention."

"Here's something fun." Rosalie jumps from the bed, opens the closet door. "Try this. See how you like it." She hands me a vibrator.

I'd never handled one before.

"Go on, play with it while I watch."

The fake penis is twice the size of Jonathan's, which is definitely bigger than Gregoire's but I'd never admit that to either of them. I touch the vibrator to my nipple and shriek as if I've been blasted with electricity.

She takes the vibrator from me and smiles. "Trust me," she says. The shocking stimulation as the dildo enters me is almost too much to bear. I fear an orgasm will come immediately and stop our fun but I don't come yet. I arch my back as Rosalie pushes the glorious monstrosity into my vagina until finally I cry out in breathlessness.

"My, my, my, aren't we having fun?" Gregoire enters the room with a huge smile, his blue eyes twinkling. "What's going on in here?" He moves to plant a quick wet kiss on my lips.

Rosalie snuggles up next to me. "Stick your ass in the air," she says.

"Just look what else I have for you." Gregoire removes a whip from a hook on the closet door. He slaps our bottoms gently. "I'll whip you naughty little girls until you beg me to stop." His smile has turned playful. "Some women like this. They have orgasms from the pain."

"Well, you're just tickling us." Rosalie scoots closer to me, turning me on my side to face her. She separates my legs with her knee. "Go away, Gregoire. Go fix us some dinner. We're right in the middle of something important." She smiles before sinking her tongue into my mouth. I lose myself in her advances. I don't hear Gregoire leave the room.

We're still at it thirty minutes later when Gregoire returns. "Can I freshen up anyone's gin? Jonathan will arrive any minute."

I hold out my glass.

"Me too but I seem to have misplaced my glass." Rosalie sits up, looks about the room.

"It's here on the vanity. Honestly, honey. I don't work for you." Gregoire picks up both glasses then swirls out of the room as if he's dressed in a flimsy evening gown.

He returns with Jonathan in tow, both naked. Both aroused. Gregoire sets the glasses on the nightstand. He picks up the whip.

"You've lost your mittens, you naughty kittens, and now you're going to cry." He cracks the whip a few times and we roll to our stomachs again as he playfully whips our bottoms several times. "See, Jonathan. We simply can't leave these two alone for one moment. They wanted to play alone. They chased me away."

"I'll handle the whip." Jonathan takes the whip and strikes our bottoms. This time it stings a bit. It also turns me on.

Rosalie moves away. She sits on the stool in front of the vanity.

"More," I say. "Give me more, Jonathan."

Each lash gets better. I enjoy the pain. "Harder." I yell. "Harder." Now I know what's been missing.

"Oh my sweet, I could never hurt you. I can only love you." Jonathan throws down the whip, mounts me from behind, massaging my hips with his huge, strong hands as he thunderously gyrates like a jackhammer.

"Deeper. Harder. Make it hurt. Make it really hurt." I yell to no avail as he explodes inside me and I'm left as empty as a butterfly's shed cocoon.

I sit alone in my townhouse in Chapel Hill. My phone rings. I expect Gregoire but it's Katie. I haven't spoken with her since the beginning of her wedding reception.

"What?" I ask when I answer.

"Shelli, it's me, Katie."

"I could see that before I picked up." Suddenly I'm sorry I answered the phone. I don't want to have a conversation with Little Miss Save the World.

"Sean and I just got back from Europe. Beka told me you weren't…that you aren't feeling well."

"What the fuck does Beka know about how I feel?"

"Can I see you? Can we talk?"

"Talk about what? Talk about my new sex life? You never want to talk sex."

"No, Shelli. I just thought I could help—"

"I don't need help. Just leave me be." I grab the end of my ponytail and wind it round and round my hand.

"But Shelli—"

"I'm fine. Really. Now go tell Beka that I said I'm fine. Stop calling me—all of you." I hear the phone go dead. Fuck. That's the first time anyone's ever hung up on me. Go to hell, Susie Homemaker.

A week of hell has passed since Rosalie, Gregoire, and Jonathan sent me home to tie up loose ends and return to New Orleans where I belong. Zack is on my case every friggin' minute. Neither Beka nor Katie will stop calling to offer their support. Support, shit. I don't listen to their pathetic messages anymore. I wonder how these people managed to fool me all these years. They're all sneaks, talking about me behind my back, spreading lies, accusing me of being rude and vulgar. Damn them all to hell. I hate them. I hate them all. Soon, I'll be rid of them forever.

Zack comes in through the garage door, jacket and tie in hand. Before he even puts them down he's running me through a plethora of questions, demanding answers, telling me what to do. My irritation with him is boiling over.

"Stop pacing. Talk to me, please." He sits at the kitchen bar where in the past we've shared intimate conversations, tried to decide how to save the world from starvation, how to revive UNC's failing football team. Such trivia. Why can't he enter the real world? People have starved since the beginning of time and they'll continue to do so no matter how many Band-Aids are handed out by goody people. And football? Who gives a shit? Get real.

"What more do you want me to say?" I throw a dishrag into the sink and glare at him.

"First I'd like to know what happened at school this week that made you decide to quit."

I feel sweat beneath my collar. "I didn't go to school. What's the use? Medicine is a useless tool in today's society."

"What made you come up with that?"

"Reality. I saw the light flicker and knew."

"Knew what?"

"That medicine is useless. People haven't stopped dying because of it. Have they?"

"Well, yes they have. Just look at the advances people like Madame Curie, Edward Salk—"

"Shut the fuck up. Madam Curie just happened to die from her research a hundred years ago. So, what else do you want to know?"

"What do you mean?"

"You said that you wanted to know about school first. What's second on your interrogation list?"

"You could wish us a happy anniversary if you had a mind to."

"Some anniversary. Two months of hell if you ask me."

"I wasn't talking about that anniversary. You don't even know what day it is, do you?"

"To hell with what day it is." I feel agitated, steamy, sweaty. I need to get away.

"Shelli, something's not right with you. Why won't you tell me?"

"Nothing is *wrong* with me. Nothing." I try to shake Zack's slime off my hands as I walk into the living room. Can't he see that he's torturing my mind? "Where's my purse? Where did you hide it?"

"It's beside the couch, where you left it. Why would I hide it from you?"

I rummage through my purse, pull out my phone. I scroll down to Gregoire.

"You're throwing your life away. Why?" Zack pleads like some wounded animal. I'm surprised he's not down on all fours.

"What life is that?" I say. Gregoire's voice mail picks up. I shake the phone.

"One more year, Shelli. You'll be a doctor in just one more year. Think about it."

I move as close to Zack's face as I can without touching him. "It's all shit, Zack. Shit." I move back a pace. "I'm a little stressed here. Can't you see that? I'm out of school. O-U-T. There are more important things in life. Like personal fulfillment."

Zack walks toward me but I back into the bathroom.

"What about your dream? Your life goal?"

"Get a life," I say, scrolling to Jonathan's name but get another voice mail. "There will never be a cure for spinal cord injuries. Never. Ben Lowenstein never walked again. Neither did Christopher Reeve, let alone get unleashed from his respirator. My research is in vain. Who am I to think I can find the secret to nerve regeneration? I'm some naïve little goody-two-shoes who can make A's without studying. It's a farce, Zack. Face it." I hold the phone against my forehead. "Shit. Think." I scroll to Rosalie. When she picks up, I slam the bathroom door in Zack's face.

"Rosalie, thank God you're home...I'm suffocating here...Yes, I'll be there tonight or tomorrow morning. I have to fly standby again...I can't wait to see you and Gregoire...I'm fine, really, just shaky...Zack? He's still here. Can you believe it? Listen, gotta go. Give my love to our boys...."

I flush the toilet while I try to think of what to say to Zack. My mind is in New Orleans. I have to get back fast.

My life, my whole future depends upon it. I flush the toilet again and plunge into the bedroom.

"Thanks for eavesdropping," I say, walking past Zack, who's leaning next to the bathroom door, his face pale, contorted. "Did you hear enough?"

"Who's Rosalie?"

"She's my new girlfriend. I fuck girls now too. How's that for honesty?"

"What are you doing to us? And why?" Zack shuffles across the room to sit on the edge of the bed. "Today is not our two month wedding anniversary. It's something more."

"Let's see, it's not Purim, it's not Hanukkah, it's not even my birthday." I say as I pull a suitcase from under the bed. "I give up. What *day* is it?"

"If you don't remember, why should I?" He turns away, grabs his coveted Tarheel basketball cap and heads for the door.

When I hear his car speed away, I shout, "Good riddance."

On my way out the door, I notice a box of handmade truffles sitting on the bar from my once favorite store, The Fresh Market. "Truffles, my favorite. How sweet. I wonder what we're celebrating." I open the box to find a gold pinky ring with two diamond chips separated by a tiny heart sitting on top of one of the truffles. "What a wimp." I say, laughing. I stick the ring into one of the truffles and throw it against the wall. The others I dump on the carpet, step on each one until they look like a pile of shit. A business card falls from the box. I pick it up to see Zack's name engraved after, Chief Project Manager. Well, well, well. Looks like Zacky-boy got a promotion, got the job of his dreams. Wonder if he had to fuck the boss? Maybe that's what we were celebrating. I flip the card over and for just a millisecond, I feel like someone else. Zack had written, *Ten years since our first dance. I love you with all my heart, Zack.* I'm taken aback. I'm fifteen.

There's the candle-lit tree house but the thought vanishes as I make my way back to Bourbon Street.

The late afternoon sun glows through the white sheers that blow out of Gregoire's apartment windows. It's hot and there's no air conditioning, just a warm breeze from a whirling rattan paddle fan. I begin to undress. My eyes wander over the gaily-decorated walls of masks. I search through the closet and discover a long blond Lady Godiva wig hanging from a hanger. I put it on and then select a mask with all purple feathers jutting out the sides. "I like this one. What do you think?"

"Very seductive, mon cher." Gregoire pulls me onto the bed. "It covers everything except your luscious lips."

He covers my mouth with his. His tongue swells like an erection as I suck it deep into my throat until we're sweaty and breathless.

"Ah, so I'm going to get my wish, am I?" I ask.

"Just what wish is that?"

"To fuck your brains out, before our friends arrive. I want you all to myself."

"I thought you liked the foursome. I thought you fancied Rosalie all to yourself."

"Oh, I do. But mostly I fancy just you."

"So, what do you like best?" Gregoire raises his eyebrows while draining the last of the gin from his glass.

"I like it all. Everything."

"You like it best when the three of us are all over you, don't you?"

"It's not enough. It leaves me wanting more."

"You don't think I'm queer, do you? I mean is that why I can't satisfy you?"

"Queer? You mean gay?" I pause, pretending to ponder the question. Tease him by making him wait for an answer while I go into the kitchen to refill our glasses. "No, I think you're a man for all seasons."

"How poetic."

"Yeah, well, that's better than bi. L'chaim." I raise my glass as I hand the other to him. After sipping it, I crawl onto the new sensuous black silk sheets, toss aside the faux cheetah skin coverlet, and snuggle my face to his. I purr like a hundred-pound cat in heat. I brush the long blond hair back, over my shoulders, exposing my erotic body. I know I'm turning him on. "So, are you going to attack me or am I going to attack you?"

"You're insatiable, Shell." He lifts his glass to his lips, rests it there while he stares at me. He takes a sip then places the glass on the lampstand beside the bed. "You really are my breath of fresh air." He leans toward me, licks the side of my face. "You surprised me."

"When?"

"At Katie and Sean's wedding."

"You mean letting you paw me in front of all those rowdy Irishmen?"

"Rowdy? Drunk they were, m' darlin'. Prudes too, especially that sissy Sean. I'm sure we had more fun on their wedding night than he did with his timid little cupcake. Were they virgins?"

"No. Why do you ask?"

"I'd like the taste of a virgin."

"What?"

"Not a child. You know I'm not into that. But I'd like to do a consentin' virgin—a fully developed woman."

"Well, I'm a fully developed shy virgin tonight." I cover my body with the long strands of the wig. "Maybe you could have your way with me." I strut beside the bed.

"Mon cher. I've been around but I've never met anyone quite like you. You're a seductress, you know."

"I'm no seductress. I'm an eighteen-year-old virgin, eager to lose my virginity."

"Oh sweet Jesus. You're on fire. I crave your hot little body, especially your firm, identical breasts with their hard upturned nipples."

"Don't you prefer men?" I ask, coyly.

"Sometimes. But sometimes, like in the case of Rosalie, I pretend that she's a young man."

"Really? With those huge breasts?"

"I just look at her hinny. She doesn't have any thighs, and her hips are narrow, like a certain young man I know."

"Jonathan?" I ask on my way out the door to fetch more gin.

"Never you mind." He holds out his glass as I fill it up. I climb back into the bed, spread my legs in front of him. "Drink up, if you want some of this." I smile.

"I do want some of that. Not Jonathan. I want my voracious virgin."

"Voracious?"

He begins to crawl toward me. We play the game. I refill the glass again and again, giving him quick, teasing glimpses of body parts. When he's polished off the fourth or fifth glass of gin and the whites of his eyes have streaks of red, I adjust the mask over my eyes, pull the long blond curls away to expose my body to his touch. I'm on my knees. I stick my finger in his mouth. When it's sufficiently wet, I remove it, sit on it then gyrate as sensuously as I know how. My body turns to fire. I grab his scrotum, hold it tight, knowing this will excite him like nothing else. "Fuck me Gregoire," I say softly, like a kitten's meow. "Fuck me now. Make it hurt. Stick that great big cock into me. I don't want to be a virgin any longer. Pound me hard. Pound me until I scream in pain."

"Pain?" He watches as I slow down my gyrations.

"Yes, pain. Right here. Pounding, excruciating pain. Then the whip."

"Shelli...."

"I want it." I scream. "Don't you dare deny me."

"I told ya I'm not into pain—gettin' it or givin' it." He jerks the mask off my face, lays spread-eagle, his erection huge, pulsating. "Jump on me, baby. Let me go deep. Cause yourself all the pain you want."

"You're ignoring what *I* want." I'm livid now. *"You* have to inflict the pain, *you."*

*"Cher,* I don't want to hurt you."

"Why? You bastard. Can't you see I need to move on to the next level? I want the whip. I need the pain."

"Are you crazy?"

"Lie still." I shout while I wrap the blond tendrils of the wig around my naked body again. I take four silk scarves from the bureau drawer. "You're going to get the royal treatment, Mr. Sebastian."

"If you don't hurry, you'll miss the action." He's squirming in the sheets, his erection growing bright red.

"Just hold back." I tie a foot to the bedpost. I'm going to give it to you like syrup—slow and sweet."

"Well, sweetheart, you're in for the ride of your life."

"A little arrogant, aren't we? Let's just get you secure for the ride. We wouldn't want you to fall off before the best part." I bend over him, brush his face with my erect nipples.

"Give me that nipple. Come on, Shell. Put that sexy little virgin tit in my mouth. Come on, girl."

"In your dreams, gay-boy, in your dreams." Slowly I straddle him, careful not to let flesh touch flesh. Just gyrate over him.

"Fuck me, you bitch. Fuck me now."

"A little angry, are we?" I let out a loud, lusty laugh. "Maybe we should call in the reinforcements early."

"And you miss taking me alone. I want to please you, Shell. Come on, I'm hurtin' here."

"You're right. I'd better be quick, my little gay-boy." I rip the wig from my head, cover his face with it. "Look at my little gay-boy who really prefers tits and pussy but is afraid to admit it. What a delightful little gay-boy you are."

He tries to shake off the wig but I wind it tighter, totally obliterating his view. I don't want to give him pleasure. This dance is for me. My body aches for the orgasm of pain. Craves it—doesn't let me think of any other thing. Slowly, I slip on him then raise and lower my body, letting him penetrate deeper than ever before, so deep that it causes the pain I need, the pain that I hunger for.

"Get this damn wig off me. I want to watch you fuck me."

"No way. I'll fuck you anyway I want. It's not you I want, bastard, it's what hangs between your legs." I move faster, stimulating myself in this dominant position. I push harder. The pain is thrilling. The pain is deeper. "No," I shout. "You came too soon. Shit. I wasn't ready. I need the pain. Don't you fucking understand? Don't you?" I rip the wig away. I slap his face over and over with both hands. "I told you to hold it. You always come too soon. You queer. I don't know why the shit I think you can satisfy me."

"Untie me, you bitch." Gregoire struggles to loosen the scarves.

"I'll untie you if you beat me, if you beat my pussy with a whip. Beat me 'til I come all over the sheets like you do."

"Just untie me, bitch. I'll make you come. I told you to go slow. You made me come. You ruined everything. Not me. Now, get these fuckin' scarves off me."

"Don't tell me what to do. Shut up. Listen to me." I glare at him.

His body shakes. I can see his rage, his passion. He looks as if he wants to rape me, penetrate me while I scream *no*. I want the same thing.

I untie his right hand. "You slut." He slaps my face hard, I lean closer. He slaps my ear. You're a little dick teasing bitch."

"Good move but you're starting at the wrong end." Quickly I loosen the remaining scarves. "You may have a big cock but it doesn't work well on girls. Just look at the pathetic thing, hanging there, undone, unable to pleasure me." When the last scarf is untied, Gregoire slaps my face hard enough to knock me down. He's almost ready, almost angry enough. I lunge at him, fingernails first, pulling strips of skin from his face and chest."

"You're a whore," he yells, as he slaps my face and ears again and again until I feel a brutal sting until I hear a loud buzz.

"You're a pathetic queer, afraid to really satisfy me, afraid to make me come the way you do."

He jumps from the bed, grabs the leather whip from the hook on the door. He turns toward me, his untamed temptress. He cracks the whip in the air once then strikes me with it. The feel of the cool leather against my hot skin excites me. I watch his penis turn thick and heavy and as red as his face.

"Again. Crack that whip against me again, bastard boy. Harder this time. Hit me like a man not a little gay-boy." Hot blood fills my head. My pleasure is about to peak. I hold back and enjoy the wrath upon my body as the whip strikes me. I'm sweating and shivering. I can barely catch my breath.

The sound of the whip sends a thrill through my groin. "That's more like it—do it right this time. No fooling around. Hurry, before Rosalie and Jonathan get here. I want to be ready for them. I want to tell them what a miserable, worthless fuck you are."

The thin leather cord approaches me in slow motion this time. I know this blow will be the one to get me going but it doesn't hit my groin. It swipes my face, breasts, belly, and thighs not once but so many times I lose count, making my desire surge. My soul screams out for more. Maybe we should have waited for an audience. Yes, an audience would be better, cheering us on, sharing my voracious appetite for the pleasures of the flesh until my vitality is gone. My arousal is beyond imagination—beyond life on earth. I am here, on the edge, enjoying every moment, wanting to come, yet not wanting this experience to end. I touch my chest then arch my back as I moan in delight. I see blood drip from my hand but there is no pain, just glorious abandon. I can't hold off for another second, I bring my feet close to my buttocks, separate my knees, exposing the tender pink skin of my perineum. The relentless stinging pain of the leather between my legs sends exhilaration through my body but calms my mind, bringing me closer to that immense feeling of total surrender, total abandonment of body and soul. Now, at last, it thunders through me. I feel as if I'm an active volcano rumbling from the depths of the earth and erupting with fiery lava that flows endlessly to the edge of the earth. Now, at long last, I am complete. I float into a peaceful unconsciousness as the lash of the angry whip continues to lull me, finally, into ecstasy.

## 12

Muted colors swirl before me. My eyelids are heavy as lead, preventing me from seeing all that is before me now. The glorious state of ecstasy has left me. My ravenous desire to be completely swept away into the most sublime state of bliss has past. I want it to take hold of me again and never let me go. Never let me feel just almost full again.

I hadn't thought about how I'd feel when the euphoria passed. Emptiness consumes me now. I don't have feelings for these people who look at me with contempt—the doctors and nurses, Zack, Beka, Katie, my parents, even my father's doctor friend, Stan Blume. I just want to feel the pleasures of the flesh, even if just for the slightest moment. I am no longer who they want me to be but a piece of jagged mirror bearing traces of a person I barely remember.

A Dr. Boutroux came a little while ago to tell me I'm a patient in intensive care at University Hospital. He asked me if I knew who beat me, if I wanted to press charges. I'm floating in a dream state. For fleeting moments, I remember my life as it once was. I close my eyes to it. That life needs to die and let me live. I don't want to remember it. I long to be back at Gregoire's, that's where I thrive, where I belong.

Time passes. I'm in and out of consciousness. My room is empty now but yesterday I saw my father and heard the cries of my mother as if she were wailing at the Wall of Jerusalem. Zack kissed my forehead. I closed my eyes to him. He is slime to me. Beka and Katie stared at me with teary, swollen eyes. I wish they would all just go away.

This morning, Dr. Boutroux changed the dressings on my face, arms, abdomen, chest, groin, and legs. I'm covered in weeping wounds but my heart is not weeping. A nurse helped me bathe what little skin that isn't swathed in white gauze then helped me out of bed. I sat in the chair awhile before she took me for a walk in the hall. That's when I saw their horrified faces—Mama, Daddy, Zack, Katie, Beka. I turned away to creep back to my bed, back into my unconsciousness.

Zack is sitting next to my bed. When he sees that I'm awake he reaches for my hand but I pull away. "I love you, Shelli. We all do," he says. "I want to take you home."

Home is the last place I want to go but I don't speak to him. I don't know what to say.

"We've all been busy the last few days." He looks so forlorn I want to laugh. "We're trying to put the pieces of this puzzle together."

I squint as if I don't understand what he's talking about.

"Ever since the night of Katie's wedding, you haven't been yourself." Zack presses on his tear ducts. "It's like you're someone else."

I stare blankly at him.

He gets up, walks across the room to the window, leans on the windowsill. Even though I can't hear his crying, I see his shoulders shake.

My father, Dr. Boutroux, and another man in a suit and tie enter the room. Zack wipes his face with a handkerchief then reaches out to shake hands. The man I don't recognize introduces himself as Dr. Muller, a colleague of Dr. Boutroux's. No one speaks and I wonder if they're waiting for me to respond to the new doctor. Their silence is freaking me out.

Finally, Dr. Muller clears his throat. He tells me that he spoke with me last night but I don't remember. He says I told him everything about Gregoire.

"Today, you don't seem to be the same carefree young woman with whom I spoke yesterday. Your family doesn't know the Shelli of the French Quarter. They only know that a man named Gregoire severely beat you with a leather whip."

"I asked him to do it."

"May I ask why?"

"Because my life is empty. I wanted to feel alive."

"Did you?" He leans forward.

"Yes, as a matter of fact, I did."

"Would you want this to happen again?"

I nod but don't look at him. I keep my eyes focused on my shaking hands.

"And end up back in hospital? Unconscious. Bleeding to death? You know you have been here for five days—the first three, unconscious and on a ventilator. You've had several blood transfusions to replace the blood you lost."

I think a while before I speak. "I want the feeling, not the bandages or the ventilator."

"Well, that's a step in the right direction." The doctor moves closer to the bed. "I've written an order to start you on Zyprexa. It's a drug that will help you feel more normal, more like yourself."

"Normal? I've never felt so normal in all my life. I don't need your drugs."

"Your family agrees that this sexual compulsivity is not a normal state for you."

"Maybe you should ask me what's *normal*."

"I'll do that tomorrow. In a week or so, when Dr. Boutroux feels that your physical wounds are healing, we'll let you go home. I've given your family the name of a colleague of mine in Chapel Hill, Dr. Anderson, a psychiatrist."

"A psychiatrist? I'm not insane, for God's sake. Why won't you and everybody else butt out of my life? Get out of my room, now. Get out."

"Think about what I've said." The doctor tips his head. "I'll speak with you tomorrow morning." When he turns to leave, he motions for Zack to follow him into the hall.

My body turns cold. Oh shit. He's a psychiatrist too. Now what? What are they going to do to me now?

Two weeks have passed and I'm sitting on the plane next to Zack. I feel a strange familiarity but I don't want to open up to him. I don't want to open up to anyone. Not even Gregoire. A great sadness fills me, like a hurricane spinning the ocean out of control, making the waters lash out at the shore it once caressed. I took the Zyprexa while I was in the hospital. The nurses made sure I swallowed it before they'd leave my room. Taking the stupid medicine was the only way I could get out of that damn place. Dr. Muller thinks I'm schizophrenic. The Zyprexa is an anti-psychotic. My mind is in a prison on an active fault. I need a drink to break out and control the shaking of it.

Endurance is nerve-wracking. Four long, stressful days, to put it mildly, have passed in Chapel Hill. I have successfully put Doctor Shelli and Mrs. Zack Levy to rest. I've moved back to my old room at home. It's absolutely amazing how easy it is to get away with murder. Every morning I flush my Zyprexa down the toilet. I'm a stranger to my family. I disgust them all, finally. Zack comes around in the evening but I feign sickness to get rid of him. After my daily sessions with the psychiatrist, I celebrate with a trip to a liquor store. I made a pact with my family that I'd only go to a psychiatrist alone. Since I can't drive yet, I take cabs. Every day a different driver. Every day a different liquor store. I can't trust a soul. No one understands that I need the gin to survive. The trust my parents have for this stranger living among them is amazing. I wonder at how they let me out of their sight.

Dr. Anderson has set up an appointment for me to meet with my peers. I see it as a last ditch effort to save me from an insane asylum. He's more perceptive than my parents. I'm pretty sure he knows about my non-compliance with the Zyprexa and gin. I think he's hoping that I'll snap out of my condition when I see how much my friends care. Too bad he's not bringing in the right friends.

The doctor's office is warm even though the blinds block the bright sun. Too many people crowd this small room, causing it to be stuffy even though I hear the hum of the air conditioning. Extra leather chairs have been brought in and all the chairs are arranged in a tight circle. I ease into a chair while Zack stands watching as if he might need to help me situate myself. He sits next to me, on the edge of the seat, looking terrified or like he may need to escape suddenly. The good doctor sits on my other side while Beka, Katie, and Sean sit like three shaking baby birds across from me.

I look at these people who are supposed to be my friends, yet I feel no connection to them. It's like I'm in a room of strangers with twisted faces, looking at me with disgust or pity or both. Briefly, I wonder who the victim is—me or them?

After Dr. Anderson introduces himself, he hands the confrontation over to Zack and then the bombardment of questions begins—all centered on what exactly happened when I got to New Orleans. When I have nothing to say, Beka breaks the silence. She tells what she says she's kept hidden to protect me. When she gets to the part of Gregoire and me at the reception, both Zack and Sean look as if they will puke. Beka goes on about my collection of the little, white wedding umbrellas from the many martinis I drank. Katie remembers our visit to the blue cottage and Miss Betsy's reaction to me. Everyone thinks I've been seized by Black Magic. I feel as if I'm the protagonist in a Stephen King novel.

The good doctor delivers a monologue on reality, morality, and I stop listening. Disgust fills my brain. What in the hell am I doing here? What do these dim-witted people want from me? "I can't take any more of this," I say, interrupting the doctor. "What's wrong with all of you? I just wanted to have a little fun." I get up to leave but Dr. Anderson catches my arm. I sit back down.

"Shelli," Katie speaks softly. "Maybe it was Gregoire. Maybe he slipped you some kind of drug at the reception and then again before he beat you."

"No," I say as emphatically as I can. "My drug screen was negative. I just had a little too much alcohol."

"So, if you just drank a little too much and had a fling, why are you acting like you hate us?" Katie's tears drip down her neck.

My body shivers in the stuffy room. Reflected deep in Katie's ocean-green eyes, I see a glimpse of my past, a glimpse of who I used to be. These heartrending eyes staring into mine touch something deep. Silence surrounds us until Katie speaks again.

"Something weird happened to you, Shelli. People don't just change. Not people like you. People who are good and kind and loving don't just suddenly become someone else. Whatever's wrong with you isn't your fault. We all have to be strong, until, until we figure everything out, until we find out what went wrong. We all love you, especially Zack, especially...me."

"She's right." Beka speaks without moving from her perch on the edge of her seat. "We love you, Shell. We love you more than you know."


I can't recall anything after Beka spoke. Somehow, I got myself to the airport and to this seat on the plane. Now there are four empty airplane bottles of Tanqueray on the tray table. When we land I dial Gregoire. A recording tells me that the number I've dialed is out of service. That God dammed Gregoire. I dial Rosalie, same recording. Fuck off. Both of you. Just fuck off you God dammed arrogant, selfish sons of bitches.

On the way to Gregoire's apartment, I have the taxi driver leave me at a liquor store down the street. Two bottles of TEN should welcome me back with open arms.

I walk to his apartment and press the buzzer. Gregoire is barricaded inside. He won't open the door.

"I'm dying out here," I say. "I need you. I need to see you. You can't believe what I've been through." I plead for some minutes before he finally cracks the door.

"They arrested me, Shelli. Those two burly policemen threw me to the ground, handcuffed me, kicked me," Gregoire yells. "Your father and husband visited me. There's a restraining order to keep me away from you. Go away. You're nothing but trouble. Stop screaming or some bitch will call the fuckin' police. Go home. There's nothing for you here. Now go." He closes the door with a bang. I hear the locks engage.

I claw at the door like an animal as I slip to the ground, groaning in my aloneness.

## 13

When they found me in the hallway the two bottles of gin were empty and I was barely alive, lying in a pool of urine, seizing my brains out. The first week in ICU is a thick fog. The doctors had me pumped full of Valium and anticonvulsants until my vital signs were stable and I could breathe without life support. I vaguely remember being loaded in a MedEvac air ambulance. A category five storm was creeping its way toward New Orleans and my father wanted me out before a repeat performance of Hurricane Katrina. The monster storm had stirred up the Gulf of Mexico with vengeance—the same way I had ripped apart everyone in my path.

Once awake, in the psychiatric ward at UNC Hospital, I endured the full throws of DTs. For the next several days, Zack and my parents sat vigil, holding me twenty-four hours a day while my body shuddered. They wiped vomit from my chin, hid my eyes to protect me from the scorpions and roaches only I could see crawling up the walls and nesting in my ears, hair, throat, and vagina. When my symptoms subsided, I fell into a deep sleep. Somewhere along the way, I'd been restarted on the Zyprexa and started on an anti-depressant.

From the moment I opened my eyes, I felt remorse worse than any sadness imaginable. Zack and my parents sat close to the bed—all with their hands on me. I touched the tangled knots of hair that swarmed my face. I asked Mama to comb them out. While she took a small brush from her purse, Zack and Daddy helped me sit up on the side of the bed. No one spoke as Mama gently brushed from the bottom up, eliminating one knot at a time. When she touched the side of my face, I pressed my head into her hand. For the first time in weeks, I felt something real from my old world.

"Daddy?"

"Yes, shayneleh?"

I smiled when he called me shayneleh. He smiled back.

"Who am I?"

"You're first a wife to Zack. You are our beautiful daughter who has been to hell and back."

I swallowed hard. "Zack?"

"Shelli," he said, as he sat next to me on the bed. He looked into my eyes then down at my hand. Gently he squeezed my hand. I squeezed back.

"Let's take you home," he said. It felt right when Zack kissed my cheek.

I thought about the hurricane that ended up fizzling out and crossing Florida as a weak tropical storm. When I thought about my recovery, I thought about Hurricane Katrina and the long recovery for the Ninth Ward. I remembered Miss Betsy telling me that I was going to be alright just as I began to spin out of control. The Ninth Ward is being rebuilt but on no safer ground. As for me, I have to raise the level of my foundations higher than the levies so that I cannot be flooded again. In the wake of this perfect disaster, new life will be delivered. Brick-by-brick, cell-by-cell. The displaced masses from the Mississippi River Delta are following a plan that I fear will lead to another disaster. I have to do better than that. I need to find a plan that will survive against every storm. I need to rebuild my life on solid ground.

Some people put a conch shell to their ear to hear the ocean. Not me. The glorious sound of the crashing waves is ingrained in the totality of my consciousness. For six days I have been here at the condo in Wilmington with Zack. This is the only reality I know right now. This place makes sense, maybe because this beach holds my first memory. The condos were brand new then—three-story structures built on stilts as close to the water as the building code allowed, twelve condos in each of four buildings. My father bought one on the north end, on the top floor with a balcony overlooking the vastness of the blue ocean with its majestic, ever-changing surf. If there's a paradise, it's right here on Kure Beach.

My teenage sister and brother screeched with delight as they ran to the edge of the sea and dove into the tumultuous waves while I stood enchanted, mesmerized, unable to move, barely able to breathe. I knew I was standing on sacred ground. I was touched, moved to tears. Mama thought I was afraid but I wasn't. I was home. Grounded. This place was mine. Every grain of fine sand, every shiny bubble in the surf, every coquina rock, every worn and broken shell belonged to me. Even the pelicans with their lofty callings and full gullets, even the snowy white seagulls that fought the wind to find their dinner—all of it, all of it was mine.

No one believes that I truly remember that day. It was then that the blue of the water blended with the blue of the sky. I bonded with that blue. I was eighteen months old. I've tried to remember what happened after that moment but my next recollection is years later.

As I watch the surf here at this place I call paradise, I'm trying to remember who I am and how, after twenty-five years of a blissfully happy privileged life, I came to be so horribly sad.

My wounds, as much as my soul, are being healed by soaking in the salty ocean. Although I brought a suitcase of clothes, I can wear only a soft cotton nightgown. The doctor removed my bandages nearly a week ago. It seems that all the stitches have been absorbed as predicted. I have not yet stood naked in front of a full-length mirror or undressed in front of Zack. The horror of the wounds on my face, neck, and arms is overwhelming enough for now, for both of us. I wonder about an intimate physical relationship with Zack. How will the scars on my breasts, belly, inner thighs, and especially my perineum affect him? We hardly speak. Nevertheless, the fact that he is here with me, holding me up emotionally, has to mean that everything will work out in time.

I need to be alone. Zack is giving me all the space I need. It's twilight now and we're sitting, a foot apart, on the same cushioned bench where I've sat a million times before to lose myself in the strength of the infinite sea. I take in a great breath of salt air and hold on to it for as long as I can. My redemption, I've decided, will be in the telling of and the letting go of my story. I touch my wedding band. Zack. What will Zack do with my sad tale? His sitting beside me should be proof of his love for me and his support. I am numb to this world. Numb to this stranger beside me. There's an emptiness in me, like I'm nothing but skin surrounding air and not even fully blown up but like a deflated helium balloon at noon on New Year's Day. Without taking my eyes off the waves, I speak. "About Gregoire..."

"Yes...?" There's a hesitated eagerness in his voice.

My breath is heavy, in and out, in and out through my mouth. I look to my fingers twisting my wedding ring, twisting this band given with love and joy and trust and my mocking it and flaunting the mocking of it. Slowly, I let flow from my cold heart all the vile, disgusting feelings that were upon me from the moment I'd arrived in New Orleans.

As I finish, I look to Zack, who is staring at a lone fisherman casting his line from the shore into the now black, moonlit sea. He hasn't flinched at my words, or turned away, or put elbows to knees and hung his head in his hands as I suspected he might. Instead, he moves his hand from his knee to the space on the bench between us. He stretches out his little finger until it presses softly against my skin at the place my thigh meets the cushion beneath it. Feeling his skin against mine eases my breathing. I stand to face him. Without saying a word, I invite him inside. I lie on the bed, still in my soft cotton nightdress and curl into my fetal position. Zack slips into the bed, outlines my body with his. I feel his warm breath seep deep into my scalp as he spins around us a cocoon of security.

The memory of the Douppioni silk of my bridesmaid's gowns surprises and comforts me. *A silk that's produced from two silkworms that spin a cocoon together,* Beka had said. Imagining the double thread, I let myself melt into Zack but trying as hard as I can, I have no strength to help with the spinning. I am content to be bound together with this compassionate man who is saving me from my madness.

Eight hours later I awake to the sound of Zack's tiptoeing in from the deck. I don't seem to have moved all night as I try to stretch my stiff body from my curled up position. Painfully, I roll to my back. Something slips from my shoulder.

"Here, I'll help you." Zack lies beside me, pulls our wedding chuppah over us. He recites the portion of our ketubah, our wedding contract, that we wrote together. "We pledge to each other to be loving friends and partners, to talk and listen, to trust and appreciate one another, to respect and cherish each other's uniqueness, and to support, comfort, and strengthen each other through life's sorrows and joys."

Tears well in my eyes. I welcome them. I begin to feel again. My numbness begins to subside and in its place is Zack's unconditional love.

"I don't deserve you," I say, turning to face him.

He takes my hand, holds it in a way I need, securely.

Zack's acceptance is beyond any conceivable logic. How can he possibly want me when I've defiled and disfigured myself so disgustingly? How can he possibly want the part of me that I so enthusiastically gave away? Would I be able to love, forgive, even *respect* him if our roles were reversed? I ponder these things as I let my hand rest in his. My mind jumbles. Telling Zack about New Orleans fills me with shame, even if I'm not the same person I was then. The sins of this other Shelli are mine. I have to embrace them. I need to learn how to let them go, how to separate myself from her. This girl inside haunts me, makes me feel sick to my stomach, disgusted, embarrassed, ashamed, lonely and alone. I don't want her to consume me ever again.

This morning the warm rays of the sun invigorate me. Zack is talking on his cell. I fear that he's being called back to work. Because of me, he lost his promotion. I should take comfort that he placed me above his career. His managers understood his dilemma. They gave him indefinite leave. When he returns to work, he'll have to begin again at the bottom of the Prague project. Low man on the totem pole. All because of me.

"That was your father, Shelli." I turn from the crashing waves to the sound of Zack's voice as he bounds down the stairs to my side. "Do you remember Stan Blume?"

"Yes, he was my father's partner before Daddy decided to teach."

"The first time you were in ICU, Stan was there, supporting your dad. He had a hunch about what had happened to you but didn't want to get your father's hopes up. Now he's pretty sure."

"What?"

"Well, it's purely speculation but your father agrees." Zack sits in the sand facing me, looking like a little boy who has just been given a basketball autographed by Tyler Hansborough or Roy Williams. "It's good news, Shell. It is." I feel my lips curl into a slight smile over Zack's enthusiasm. "Your dad said he's been up all night checking articles in medical journals, talking to medical colleagues and psychiatrists all morning."

"So, what is it? Tell me." I reach out to take his hands in mine. It feels right to touch this man I am supposed to be one with.

"Alcohol-Induced Psychosis."

Hearing the words turn my world darker. I try to speak but my jumbled mind can't make a complete thought. I let go of Zack's hands and wrap my arms around myself.

"It's alright. Listen to this." He pulls a scrap of paper from his shirt pocket. "The sudden consumption of alcohol in large quantities by someone without a history of mental illness can precipitate a personality disorder similar to schizophrenia."

"Schizophrenia. I was messed up but I never lost touch with reality—or maybe I did."

"Don't worry about that part right now. As it stands, schizophrenia is the diagnosis the psychiatrist gave you. Stan said that maybe psychosis is a better term. Listen to me. It's curable. There's a doctor in Raleigh who concurs with Stan. They both think he can help you make a full recovery in less than a year, maybe even in as few as three months."

I reach to catch my tears.

"Shelli, are you happy or sad? Nod if you're happy." Zack is on his knees now, leaning toward me.

I nod. We hold each other and we cry together until I catch my breath. "So, I'm not going crazy?"

"No, you schnook, you are not going crazy. You won't ever go crazy as long as you lay off the alcohol." Zack moves out of the hug but keeps hold of my arms.

"I can do that. I've never had a substance dependency until—"

"You don't have one now."

"How did I get it before? Why did I suddenly crave the gin?"

"I'm not sure, baby. Maybe it was always there but you had such a low tolerance for it that you never drank enough for it to cause a problem."

"I've always drunk wine and champagne. I never had a problem—not even a headache or hangover." I shake my head. "Was it just the gin? I mean if I drink gin again, will the psychosis come back?"

"Your father said it's a possibility."

"I don't want or need any alcohol now. I never really did need it until I got to New Orleans."

"Everything happened at once—the stress of the wedding, the shock of Naomi's death, the reality of my job, even the disappointment of going to Katie's wedding alone."

"The stress of our wedding was healthy stress."

Zack stops to think. "What about Naomi—maybe you didn't get to grieve properly. I'm no doctor but maybe that's where you need to begin."

"What was it about the gin? One taste, I went out of control. Why did I drink that first drink? Why did I crave more after the first swallow?"

"I'll leave that one up to the psychiatrist or your dad. I've always heard from college buddies that gin isn't good for women, makes them horny enough to want sex from a fire hydrant."

Hearing that deepens my sadness. I'm ashamed. I close my eyes, try to forget the menagerie of New Orleans. "There's one thing that's bothering me. While I was…sick, the gin didn't dull my senses, it heightened them. But now, it's as if I'm seeing that world through someone else's eyes, like reading a novel or watching a movie."

"The doctors will help you deal with everything." Zack smiles. I see the wrinkles on his forehead ease.

"Yeah." I try to smile. "I'm a little achy. Let's go inside. I want to call Daddy, let him know I'm ready to do whatever it takes."

Once inside I sit on the side of the bed and hold Zack's phone with both hands. "I know this is something I have to do alone but I need you to hold me. Not just today…always."

"There's no place I'd rather be than beside you."

Settled into Zack's embrace, I lift the phone to my ear. Daddy answers expecting Zack but sounds thrilled to hear it's me. Mama has to say hello too. There's joy in their voices. I wipe tears of happiness on Zack's shirt.

The evening air embraces us in a balmy blanket as we watch, in silence, the blue of the waves turn to gray while the sun streaks the low clouds in bright gold and deep pinks.

"Can you, will you, forgive me?" I say. "I've broken every vow. I'm so, so very sorry."

"Yes, I forgive you. To be honest, I didn't think I ever could. I didn't know what was happening. I was angry. The thought never occurred to me that you weren't in control. I didn't want you to stop loving me. I was jealous and hurt."

The tears that continue to linger just below the surface of my consciousness splash against my cheeks. I want this forgiveness to ease my guilt, erase my sadness but it doesn't. I haven't hurt just Zack, I've hurt everyone. Zack tells me that it wasn't me—it was someone who's gone from our lives. I try to believe him but I know that girl, I am that girl. I remember everything I said and did. I know that Zack loves me unconditionally but I worry about Beka and Katie. How can I ever mend things with them? Then there's Gregoire. I brought evil to his world. If he was arrested because of me, Jonathan probably fired him. I feel as if I can't exhale before the next gasp knocks me down. I have to will my mind to stop rehashing, to stop remembering.

Zack and I stay snuggled up on the deck until midnight. Even though my psychosis is behind me, I know that the other horrible, despicable Shelli, still lingers close to my surface and will emerge if I let my guard down for one second. I can't trust anyone, especially myself.

## 14

I slept until nine-thirty this morning. I had hoped to start my recovery with a sunrise walk on the beach but the sun is already high in the sky. The waves stir the sand at my feet. I try bending to touch the warm water but my body stings when I try, so I stoop painfully, for as long as I can stand it then right myself again to ease the pain.

So much has happened in the nine weeks since Naomi died. Zack thinks that my psychosis began with Naomi's death so soon after our wedding. I empty myself of the present and imagine the taxi ride returning us home from our honeymoon. It's difficult to remember such happiness.

I recall my sunburned back sticking to the vinyl seat, Zack's fingers inching up my thigh, pulling my sundress with it. I pressed my hands on Zack's to get him to stop teasing me. When we got home, it seemed new somehow, like the rings on our fingers had changed an ordinary townhouse into a sacred home. Unopened wedding gifts were stacked against the walls like wallpaper. We abandoned our luggage in the middle of the living room floor then romped gaily to the bedroom where we celebrated making love as husband and wife in our own bed. We had one more day before Zack had to return to work so we stretched out our honeymoon for as long as possible.

We spent the next day opening our gifts and snacking on junk food between magnificent interludes of lovemaking. When Zack went to work a few days before I had to return to school, I prided myself in being a housewife—tidying up, washing clothes, putting our gifts away, and experimenting with gourmet dinner recipes. I was happily married. In those few days my heart was so light, so buoyed up that I had to hold onto it to keep it from floating away…until Mama called, barely able to speak of our great loss. I knew Naomi was dead before she spoke a word.

People have gathered along the water's edge with their beach chairs and sunscreen, so I walk south past the last of the condos then along the path that separates me from the ocean by huge boulders brought in to thwart the beach from eroding into extinction. I turn to see how far I've come then decide I have enough energy to trudge on. When I turn, I see that my footprints have been erased by the water-soaked shore—as I was erased by a power stronger than my own will. Finally, past the hordes of people sunbathing, playing volleyball, and collecting shells at the public beach at Fort Fisher, I share a long stretch of empty beach with just the dunes. I drop my beach towel on the shore. Without removing my nightgown, I enter the ocean. I imagine holding Naomi on my hip, listening to her laughter as we jump the waves, making our way to the calm water, past where the waves break on to the shore. I lay Naomi on her back supporting her with my hands until she trusts me enough to float alone. I float next to her holding her tiny frail hand. "My beautifulists Naomi. Come to me now. Let me feel your presence."

An ache develops in my side. I concentrate on it as it worsens and moves to my heart. "Please don't bring an ache, Naomi." The ache worsens until I feel I'll drown. I make my way to the shore, crying and coughing up saltwater. I fall to the sandy earth. "My beautifulists Naomi. My beautifulists Naomi," I cry aloud. Tears sting my eyes, blur my vision. I watch them sink into the sodden ground. I'm unable to stop the gasps or ease the aching. Sand is irritating my wounds, making them bleed as my heart is bleeding. I see the casket, see Naomi's lifeless, blue body wrapped in a shroud. My brother's wailing fills me as the rabbi rips his shirt. I see the blank stare in Rachel's swollen, red eyes. I feel the pain of death. "Why Naomi? Why not me?"

A cloud covers the sun. I feel cold, alone, alienated by this so-called-god of love who maims and murders children.

My chest heaves, I can't stop the flood of tears. I remember the funeral where friends recited the traditional condolence, Hamakom y'nachem etchem, b'toch sh'ar availai tziyon ee yerushalayim—May God comfort you among all the mourners of Zion and Jerusalem. I try to feel the comfort but still the ache in my heart threatens to undo me. I try to think of a prayer or poem or song but nothing comes to mind except the mikvah the week before my wedding. I decide to hold a mikvah for Naomi. I slowly make my way back into the ocean, feeling the waters healing my grief as I immerse myself deeper into the blue. I allow the waters to attend to the parts of my body that feel the most grief—my empty arms, my aching heart, my lips that kissed her forehead on the last day I saw her. I continue the immersions. As I rise to the surface for the last time I see an image of a robust Naomi smiling, handing me a translucent blue drape that wraps me in the possibility of joy and hope.

After rinsing the sand from my gown I wrap the towel around my shoulders and head back to the condo. As my feet slap the wet sand a lightness of heart encompasses me.

"You're about to miss breakfast," Zack calls from the deck.

"I'll be right up. I want to shower down here. The sand is caked to me."

Before I finish washing off under the showerhead attached to the side of the building, Zack stands beside me with a clean towel. I turn my back to him. When I shut the water off, I look down at my scarred body. Zack's hands tenderly touch my arms as he turns me around. No emotion shows on his face as I reach for the towel in an attempt to cover my disfigurement. Zack pulls me to him. He weeps into my wet hair. He doesn't speak. I wonder what this silence means. At last he steps back then wraps me in a towel as tenderly as he would wrap a baby for sleep. He looks at me, his hazel eyes brimmed in red and I see a calmness, a relief that hasn't been there since this nightmare began.

"Well, Dr. Segal-Levy, it looks as if the patient is healing nicely."

"So many scars."

"Healing scars on a sensational body." Zack smiles. "I bought half-a-dozen egg biscuits from The Old Pier House to fatten you up. Come on while the coffee's hot."

Zack takes my hand. I follow him up the stairs. My heart is beating wildly.

The coffee tastes good and it warms me. I savor every bite of the biscuit that fills a hunger I hadn't noticed until now but just one is enough. I sip at the coffee while I tell Zack about my morning and that he was right about starting my healing process with Naomi. I tell him that I'm glad he's seen my scars and when he's ready I'll show him the worst ones. He wants to see them now, when I finish my coffee. I realize that everything has been about me. Even though I'm not so sure I want Zack to see the deepest wounds that haven't turned to healing scars yet, I know that this is something I must do, for him, for his healing. When I take the last swallow, I lead him to the bedroom. We open the drapes to let in the bright sunlight. I get the gooseneck lamp from the desk and a hand mirror from the bathroom. I lie back on the bed.

Zack is silent as he studies the intricate lines of stitches that look like a highway map over swollen red tissue. I hold the mirror to see what he sees. Without a word, he takes the lamp and mirror away, then lies facing me on the bed. I turn as he pulls me to him. We cry until his whole body shakes and deep moans escape his throat. This crying and holding on for dear life goes on until we fall asleep in each other's arms.

We awaken to the ring of Zack's phone. He holds me tighter. "Just let it ring," he says. "I love you, Shelli. I love you more today than I've ever loved you."

I'm aware of the slight smile creeping onto my face. I can't remember the last time I've smiled. "We haven't talked about you, Zack."

"We just did." He readjusts his pillow.

I roll over to ease my back close to his chest. "There's so much I have to get over." I want to hide my sadness from him. "What if I can't tell the psychiatrist what I've told you? What if I can tell him and he can't offer a cure? What if—"

"Shhh, you don't have to worry so much. My mom once told me something that Jesus said to the Jews or the Jews said to Jesus. Something like, "Physician, heal thyself." Well, I think you're doing a fine job, Dr. Shelli."

"But what if I don't have what Stan thinks I have? What if I wake up tomorrow, go buy a bottle of gin, and a plane ticket to some godforsaken place? What if—"

Zack rises up on an elbow. He lets out an exasperated sigh. "Stop, Shell. No more what-ifs. One day at a time, okay?"

"Right." I roll back over to face him. My arm and chest hurt too much to lean on my elbow like he is. "Today has started out so well. I think I'm ready to go home."

"How about tomorrow morning?"

"Sure." Home. I close my eyes, see our home in a new light. Warm, serene—the way it's supposed to be. A place for me to heal.

"I think I'd like to go back to work on Monday," Zack says.

"Are you sure you're ready? I mean everyone knows I went off the deep end with a sex maniac and ended up in an insane asylum. Can you handle that?"

"I can handle anything if I know you'll be beside me forever."

"Zack." I lean my face next to his, brushing my eyelashes against his cheek. "That ring you bought me for the tenth anniversary of our first dance…."

"The one in the truffles box."

"Yeah." I hold my breath, will myself not to cry again. "Can you forgive me for…"

"Yes, I've already forgiven you."

"When?"

Zack strokes my hair. "When the DTs were over. The way you looked at me was like old times."

"Old times?" I ask slowly.

"Your spark came back. I knew I was looking at my wife, the woman I'd loved for as long as I had memory, the woman I've loved since before time."

"I felt it too. Just at that moment. Alcohol had to be the cause of my psychosis. As soon as the alcohol was out of my body, I felt like me again—except for the sadness."

"Hush, now." Zack nuzzles his face next to mine.

"Do you still have it? The ring?"

"Yes, I still have it."

"Will you give it to me when we dance again?"

"I'll give it to you even if we never dance again."

We stop to see Mama and Daddy on our way home. Their worried expressions have eased but they've aged. Mama hugs me to her as we sway in silence. I nest against her heart like a frightened baby bird. Tucking against my mother's beating heart is exactly what I need. My left arm stings with pain, as do my breasts and hips as I cling to her, not caring about the pain. I just care about the love, the love I so desperately need right now. I try to shut out the girl inside who shames me so. Before I can think, I catch Daddy's blissful stare. "Why?" I shout. "Why do I have to take pills to be me?" Mama clings to me tighter, her hands pulling me closer. I feel her grief. "Why was I invaded by an alien? Why?"

Daddy takes a step closer to me, cocks his head slightly. He is calm, calm like a ship sailing steady on a tranquil sea. "Shayneleh, we see you and we know you. This alien, she was not you. You are not responsible for her. We celebrate you."

"But I've hurt you. I've hurt all of you."

"Shayneleh, it's nothing, a little scar only. It is healing well. Our daughter has come back to us. Thanks be to God."

Monday has come too soon. I'm glad that my appointment with Dr. Sloan is at nine-forty-five. I don't think I could stand it if I had to wait until late afternoon. Mama has agreed to drive me and I'm glad she'll be along for moral support. I smile when it occurs to me that she's probably been up all night worrying. This probably isn't the first night she's worried for one of her children all through the night. I see her car and head out the door.

"Good morning, darling," she says as I climb into the seat beside her.

"It's going to be fine, isn't it?" I keep my eyes fixed on hers as I shut the door.

"Yes. It's going to be fine."

"Mama, remember how happy we were at my shower? Remember how I held you and said I'd never let you go? I'm going to say it again. I'll never let you go, Mama. Never."

"I know, darling. You never really let me go. You never did."

"Thanks, Mama. Thanks for saying that."

We drive on in silence. Mama glances at me and smiles as if she could take this burden from me. I feel sick to my stomach. The orange juice I had for breakfast refluxes into my esophagus. "Stop the car." I hold my hand over my mouth. Mama pulls to the side of the road just in time for me to open the door. I vomit into a ditch. Mama pulls a Kleenex from her purse. "Sorry, I should have had a piece of toast with the OJ."

"Shelli. You have nothing to be sorry for. Nothing."

I press my lips together. I can't even force a smile. We don't speak again until we search for the right street then the right building. My stomach begins churning again when we pull into the parking space.

Mama squeezes my hand when the receptionist calls my name. I take in a deep breath and follow her to a small room with three easy chairs separated by two end tables. The walls are olive green. The lamps on the tables have warm burnt orange shades that comfort me. Dr. Sloan introduces himself and invites me to sit wherever I please.

I sit in a chair adjacent to him with a view of tall shrubs with tiny white flowers outside the window. He has no chart or papers or tape recorders. We talk in a professional, friendly manner. My answers to his questions tell him, briefly, the story of my life. I'm surprised that he doesn't ask specific details of New Orleans and that he doesn't say, "I see," or ask me how I feel about this or that. The longer I talk, the more comfortable I feel. My answers become more detailed. There's a lull in the conversation, I look at my watch—eleven-fifteen. I'm surprised. I've been here over an hour. It seems like I just got here a few minutes ago.

"Shelli." The doctor looks at me in earnest. "I don't believe you realize that you've already begun the healing process. You're right to question the substance dependency. If you take a drink and the psychosis returns, we'll have a definitive diagnosis. But it might kill you. Right now we're speculating. One drink could cause you to want another and another until your whole world spins out of control. It's up to you to admit that you have a dependency. You've been in ICU twice with blood alcohol levels that should have killed you. You might not be so fortunate the next time."

Dr. Sloan stands, shakes my hand, and says I can sit here for as long as I wish. If I need assistance, I should push the button on the wall.

His words anger me. I sit rigidly. My mind is on fire. Anger turns to rage. Why? Why didn't I die? Why did Naomi die? How could I hurt Zack, be unfaithful, be utterly wretched to him? How could I ruin Katie's reception? How could I swear at Beka and Mama and Zack when they tried to reach out to me? Why did I want to do all the disgraceful things I did? I feel a stirring deep in my pelvis, a wicked yearning to return to my psychotic past, to get away from all the people I've hurt. I don't have the strength to deal with this garbage. Why did I suddenly need, really need alcohol and noxious sex? Why couldn't I get enough to satisfy me? Why? Why won't this fucking doctor tell me why? Naomi's death started this. Her death ruined my happiness, began my downward spiral. Then Zack... No. This kind of thinking makes me shatter. I try to see myself as I once was but the image skews, elongating my face, twisting my trunk, contorting my extremities until I'm nothing more than a tainted mass of color. The stirring in my stomach turns to a ball of stone, bouncing from side to side, punching at my kidneys, rising to engulf my heart and throat then from the depths of my being comes a scream so loud and so long that I think it will triumph over me. When the scream is just an echo in my head another takes its place—louder, deeper, longer. I scream until I'm spent. I lie on the floor, curled in my fetal position, shaking, sweating, trembling. The screams let loose the horrors that have ravished my mind. It is now I decide my fate. I gather myself together and dry my eyes.

The sound of the front door opening awakens me from a dazed sleep. I open my eyes to darkness, realizing that I have no sense of time. Zack calls my name. The tone of his voice adds to my disorientation. When he flips on the overhead light, I squint at the brightness. "What's wrong?"

"Tell me about the gin," he says. His face is ashen.

"Oh, that." I run my fingers through the tangled mess my hair is in, gingerly stretching my sore body. "Help me up and I'll show you." I take Zack's hand and lead him through the kitchen into the back yard. On the way, I pick up a small bottle of gin.

Earlier, I had arranged kindling in a little pile in our hibachi. I hand the gin to Zack, set the twigs on fire then take in a big breath. "I have an alcohol dependency. I will always have it. So, this is what I'm going to do with alcohol from now on." While the fire grows red hot, I pour the entire bottle of gin into a cast iron skillet, place it on the grill, and quickly stand back. We watch in silence as the simmering gin begins to steam and then explodes into fierce flames. I feel a validation of my earlier primal scream.

"Remember at Naomi's funeral I told you about this scream I had inside? That if I could only get it out I'd feel better? Well, I kept feeling that scream but it wouldn't come out. I could weep but still no scream. I think the repressed scream was the beginning of the psychosis. The longer I kept it in, the more psychotic I became. I'm not denying the alcohol dependency. I'm accepting it. I think holding back that scream weakened me, depressed me and the alcohol blocked it. The alcohol made me do the terrible things I did. But it was me who raised every single glass and bottle to my lips. No one forced me. I did it of my own free will. I'm guilty as charged." I grimace. "I must have been in a sound-proof room."

"What?"

"At the doctor's office. I screamed so loud. It should have upset the whole building."

Zack nods.

"In Dr. Sloan's closing statement he praised me, accused me, threatened me, challenged me, and left me angry as hell. When he left me alone in the room, I felt like I was going to burst if I didn't scream my guts out. When it was over, I lay sobbing on the floor then just like that," I say clicking my fingers, "I was over it. It was like the scream sealed the past, opened the future. The room seemed brighter, as if the sun suddenly emerged from a storm."

"An ecstatic experience?" Zack holds my shoulders.

My lower lip is quivering. "Maybe. Everything seemed so clear. I knew exactly what I had to do."

Zack lets his hands slip down my arms to take hold of my hands. "That's my girl."

"You'd better call Mama and tell her that I didn't drink the gin."

"She knows about it?"

"She drove me to the liquor store." I smile. "I told her my plan. She trusted me."

"You earned her trust."

I sigh. "Can you believe it?"

"Knowing your mother, absolutely yes." He brings my fingers to his lips.

"So, what is an ecstatic experience anyway? Was I simply impassioned or overcome with emotion or was it from some higher power?"

"You're the only one who can decipher that one."

"I have this feeling that maybe God wants to forgive me, if there even is a god. Everything's so confusing. Why do people…why do I call out to God when I'm in trouble? It's like there's this special pocket that I can pull God out of when I need help."

"When things are good, people don't need a god to save them." Zack holds my stare.

"Maybe you're right. I feel a tug to believe like my parents do. Like Saphira and Sol do. But nothing makes sense."

"It doesn't make sense to me either." Zack hangs his head but keeps a tight grip on my hands. "Maybe it will someday."

"The only things I know for sure are that I need to believe what Daddy said, that I'm not responsible for the acts of the alien."

"Your father's right." Zack lets go of my hands, walks to the edge of the dwindling fire, and sits on the ground. His sudden silence frightens me.

I roll a log with my foot to the place next to where he sits but I don't sit on it. "What's wrong? Tell me, Zack, please."

He is sobbing now. I sit on the log, my hand on his knee. I stare at the fiery embers that blur through my tears. I wait for him to speak.

Finally, he pulls a handkerchief from his back pocket, wipes his face. "I guess I needed to do that as much as you needed to scream. When you poured your heart out at the beach, I felt like you were back and the horror was over. Even though I'd pieced the story together while you were still in New Orleans, I didn't really believe it until you told me everything. I think I got angrier after thinking about what really happened. I couldn't imagine you with another man, two men, a woman, even. Especially all four of you together. I didn't understand what had happened to you." Zack looks away. "I didn't want to believe what you said was true. I was angry but more than that. I was jealous, left out. When I came home tonight to a dark house and found the gin, I thought you'd left me again."

"Jealous?" I'm taken aback. "Jealous how?"

Zack's expression scares me. "Other men were having their way, having their sadistic fun with you while I sat home alone."

"It wasn't about wanting to do what I did. How can you be jealous?" My sadness has taken a turn—it has cut deeper. "I never meant to hurt you. I still don't understand everything but I do comprehend one thing."

"What's that?"

"That you were there, beside me, both times I was on the ventilator. You were there when I cursed you. You were there holding me up through the DTs." I stop to catch my breath and dry my burning eyes. "Will we ever be able to forget the debauchery?"

Zack stands, picks up the empty gin bottle, and heaves it against a rock with all his might. He speaks deliberately. "Your escapades were a fantasy that has ended."

"Can you ignore them, forget them?" I ask fearing the answer.

"I'm trying, Shell." He's calmer now. "You're helping me to forget. You've just killed the alien."

I try to believe that one day we *will* forget everything. Right now we're haunted—both of us. Zack takes my hand in his. He doesn't smile. He's so wounded. We need to recover, we need to forget. We need to remember our happy times. We need to make new memories, happy memories.

"I'm ready to call Beka and Katie—that is, if you're certain they want to hear from me."

"Believe me. They're both sitting by the phone, waiting for your call."

"That's so nice to hear." I try to believe what Zack is telling me is true. "I'll call first thing tomorrow. In the meantime, will you dance with me tonight? I may not be able to go all the way but I want to try to please you."

He pulls me to him. I feel his hesitation. I thought my suggestion would be welcomed but he's not thrilled the way I thought he would be. I'm spoiled goods. I know it. He knows it. He backs away and smiles.

Without speaking we extinguish the fire with sand and water from the garden hose then head for the house.

I force my words. "Mama brought some chicken soup. We can warm it up now if you want."

"Okay." Zack kicks off his shoes. "Why don't you call your mother first. Tell her about our celebration. She needs to know that you didn't drink the gin."

So much for the progress I made today. I can't help but stare at Zack. He can't stand the thought of touching me and Mama's sitting home expecting a distress call.

After dinner, Zack catches me off guard. He comes to me and for the first time since the night before he left for

Prague, he touches my waist, lets his hands slip up under my shirt. I try to focus on his needs, not the scars he's touching. He surprises me by kissing my lips, my neck, by removing my camie. Confused, I pull his shirt from his trousers. His arousal excites me in an old familiar way but the memory of my euphoric orgasm in New Orleans thunders in the background. Before I can get to skin, he picks me up, carries me to our bed, and sets me down on soft cotton sheets. I participate in this event even though fear grips me. While Zack unleashes his passion, I realize that I've mistaken my desire. I don't want it to be like this. I fear he desires to be with the Shelli of New Orleans, that he's aroused by my escapade, aroused by more than one partner. Does he want to dominate me? Rape me? Does he want me to be aggressive, kinky? I try not to pull away. I'm not ready for this after all but I continue my masquerade. My tears dampen the pillowcase. My breath comes from deep within. I'm relieved that my wounds prevent us from intercourse. My mind is invaded with dark visions of New Orleans, of sweaty body parts, of being slammed into a grimy bathroom wall by a stranger. Do I want Zack to be rough with me? Does he want to hear me scream in pain? I try to focus on Zack, his needs, his fears. I live for Zack's loving touch, yet wonder if he's acting out the part of the loving, accepting husband when, in fact, he loathes all the horrible things I've done and wants to punish me for them. When he's spent, he runs a finger across my lips. "I adore you," he says. I close my eyes to escape this madness and we doze off.

When we awaken, Zack reaches across me into a drawer beside the bed. He slips the gold ring with the entwining hearts and little diamond chips on the little finger of my right hand. "Thank you for the dance. You were wonderful."

"But we didn't go all the way, I mean we didn't have…"

"We made love. We danced."

I swallow hard and look at the ring. "It's gorgeous. I was a fool to do what I did."

"It's over, Shell. Happy tenth anniversary of our first dance. Tonight was even better than the first one."

I hide my face from Zack, realizing that my earlier primal scream was nothing more than a hoax. I force my body and my mind to go numb.

## 15

Before Zack awoke this morning I was up, showered, and had coffee made. Even though I don't quite know what to make of Zack's reaction to my illness as jealousy, I have to think that we've made progress. At least the larger scheme of things looks clearer today. What is it they say, that the morning is wiser than the evening? I realize that I have a way to go in my therapy. I'm fragile and paranoid. Being able to accept that seems to be as big a step as admitting that I'm an alcoholic.

My phone is in my hand but when I scroll down to Beka's name, my thumb won't hit dial. I want to call Katie too before they get off to work but I'm afraid of the reaction. What if they're not waiting for me to call? I sip the coffee feeling my stomach churn. Coffee, like orange juice, doesn't sit well on an empty stomach, especially a nervous, empty stomach. I pop a slice of bread in the toaster then wait with knife in hand to spread butter and strawberry jam. I look at the clock on the microwave. Five fifty-five. It's a sign. Three fives. Five is supposed to be a lucky number. Before the toast pops up, I scroll to Beka's name again and hit dial before the time changes to five fifty-six and I lose my nerve.

Beka answers before I'm sure the call went through. She screams into the phone—she's that excited to hear from me. We talk about me, the psychiatrist, Zack, and my parents. I feel relieved. When she cries I begin to understand the toll my illness has had upon her and how she has shaken it off before I offer one word of apology.

"If you're up to it, I'd like to drive down Sunday afternoon. I have a show this weekend but should be able to get away by about three or so." Her voice softens and slows until I get the feeling she's afraid I'll say no.

"Are you certain? Of course." I'm trying not to sob. My breath catches. I can't continue.

Beka's blubbering too, so I guess we're alright—the slobber sisters, two of us at least, have reunited.

My sobs turn to giggles. As Beka rambles on, my heart beats faster thinking about her bounding through the front door.

"There's something else," Beka says just before we hang up. "Some good news but I want to tell you in person."

"Don't do this, Beka. Tell me."

"It's a long story, a very juicy, long story that can only be told in person."

"Is it a man?"

"That and more. You'll see. Give my love to Zack."

I let out a loud huff and know that Beka is smiling at my suspense.

"That sounded like it went well." Zack shuffles out of the bedroom rubbing his eyes, hair in disarray, totally nude with a semi-erection protruding in front of him. "Any chance you want to play before the fun goes away."

"Play? Sure but later." I force a grin, happy that I have an excuse *not* to play. "If I don't call Katie this instant, Beka will call her to spoil my surprise."

"Women." Zack shakes his head. I push him gently back into the bedroom. "I'll hold you to that, missy," he says climbing back into bed. My phone beeps then dies. I realize I've forgotten to recharge it. I find Zack's on the table by the bed, scroll to Katie's name, hit dial.

"Top O' the morning to ya. This is Sean."

"Top of the morning to you too, Sean. This is Shelli."

"Shelli! Hello. I thought it was Zack."

"I'm on Zack's phone." I smile. "I just wanted to call to let you know I've returned from the dead and plan to stick around for a while."

"Sounds like you've been through hell."

"Well, it wasn't the best time of my life. I know I put you and Katie through hell too. I just want to say how sorry I am, for...for everything."

"It's not your fault, Shelli. It's tragic what happened to you. Zack says you're handling it well."

"I'm trying. Still, there are these memories. I feel so sad for hurting you and Katie and everyone else. I can't tell you how sorry I am. I called to beg your forgiveness."

"Beg? We'll have none of that. We forgive you, you don't need—"

"Stop at that. That's all I need. Just to hear that. Thanks, Sean. I need to hear it from Katie too. Is she there? How is she? Will she want to talk to me?"

"She's in the shower. She's going to squeal in delight when I hand her the phone."

"Just tell her I called. Have her call back when she's out of the shower."

"She'll never forgive me for that, speaking of forgiveness. I'm walking to the bathroom now. Hold on."

"Kate, my love, there's a call for you."

I can hear water running and Katie's sweet, muffled voice. "I can't take it now. I have shampoo in my hair. Who is it?" Katie sounds irritated.

"You'd better take this call. It's one you don't want to miss."

"Is it Shelli? Give me the phone."

"Hi, Katie, it is me. It's Shelli."

"Shelli, Shelli. I can't believe it. It's so good to finally hear from you. I miss you so much. I need to see you right now."

"Wow. What a reception. I miss you too."

"Can I come over? I mean as soon as I get dressed? I just need to see you in person."

"Of course you can come over but won't you be late for work?"

"I have to meet a client at the Hilton in Chapel Hill at eight-forty-five. I'm free until then. Please say yes. Please."

"Yes, Katie. I'll be waiting. Now go rinse the shampoo out of your hair. The coffee's already on."

"I'll see you in half an hour. I'm so happy. I love you."

At least I don't bawl until I hang up. I sit on the edge of the bed and let it all out.

"Shelli?" Zack turns over to face me. "Nod if you're happy," he says.

I nod and blow my nose. The tears keep flooding. When I catch my breath, I blow out a big sigh. "That's everyone. I've apologized to everyone."

"Now, come here. Let's celebrate."

How can I turn such a marvelous guy away, especially when I can see his excitement growing? I take in a few slow, deep breaths and force a smile.

Zack pulls my nightgown off over my head. I lean over him letting my nipples brush his lips then kiss him from head to belly, stopping to play with his erection, which is at attention now. It doesn't take much for a young man who's been celibate all this horrible time to explode in ecstasy after a few seconds of sensual touch. He laughs at the semen that's splashed on my face, pulls me to his side, covers me with kisses. He loves me and I realize that with every look, every touch, every phone call he's addressing this need I have to know that I am loved, that I am acceptable, and that I am forgiven. I lie still, trying to let his enthusiasm seep into me but my mind repeats the words, *spoiled goods, spoiled goods.*

"You're wonderful," Zack says, touching my cheek with his index finger. "I'm going to be singing' in the rain today."

"You'd better start your singing in the shower or you'll be late."

Zack kisses my neck before rolling out of bed. I feel like an actress on a stage.

After Zack leaves for work, I pace from the kitchen to the living room while I wait for Katie. It's gloomy outside, just beginning to sprinkle. Something is comforting about the gloom. Maybe because I can turn the lamps on and burn candles during the day, giving the place a comforting glow. I light a candle on the bar and another on the coffee table. When I blow out the match, I hear Katie's car pull up. I swing the front door open. She runs to me with arms wide. We stand in the doorway hugging, rocking, and crying for the longest time. We don't need to explain or question or talk just yet. The closeness heals. We're lost in each other's love and acceptance and happiness.

"Come in," I say as we both, at last, step back a pace.

"You look great." Katie looks me over. "The scars aren't nearly as bad as I'd imagined. They're almost healed, aren't they? When the redness goes away, I bet they'll disappear." Katie takes my hands in hers, turns me side-to-side. "They're just on the front, aren't they?"

"The ones you can see are on the front but the worst ones are on my bottom—there's a different kind of scar inside." I shrug my shoulders.

"So, what does the doctor say?" Katie hangs her purse on the door handle then shakes the rain from her ringlets.

"Which one, the surgeon or the psychiatrist?"

A grimace overcomes Katie's radiant face. She looks to the ground.

"It's okay. I'm seeing both. I need both. Look at me, Katie."

Slowly she lifts her sad eyes to meet mine.

"The scars on the inside, the mental scars, are worse than the physical ones. But this week has been healing for all the scars. Your hug just healed half of them."

"We've been so worried."

"I'm so sorry for all the pain I brought to all of us."

"It wasn't your fault."

"So many people have told me so. I'm beginning to believe it. Come, we need to talk over coffee, like we always have." I surprise myself by not saying *like we used to do.* Maybe there's hope for me yet.

"Do you have milk?"

"Sure, why?"

"On our honeymoon in France, we drank coffee with steamed milk, about half a cup of each. I can't drink it any other way now."

I take the milk from the fridge. "How do you warm it? In the microwave or a saucepan?"

"A saucepan is best. Just bring it to a simmer. Let it stick to the sides of the pan."

"I'll try some too. I want to hear all about your honeymoon. Did you bring pictures?"

Katie sighs as she pulls out a barstool. "My honeymoon was the last thing on my mind after you called. We have a beautiful album from the professional photographer. I'll bring it over—"

"Sunday night, if you want. Beka's coming late Sunday, probably by ten-thirty or eleven. Has she seen them?"

"Not yet. She's just seen the photos on Facebook— they're snapshots posted by people who attended the wedding." Katie's voice trails off as she turns from me to look out the window for a moment. Slowly her gaze meets mine. "I don't mean to sound dreadful but when Beka was here last time, we were so upset over you that we didn't talk about anything else."

"I'm sorry, Katie." A twinge in my heart makes me realize that I've ruined more than just her wedding reception. Because of me she didn't get to bask in the happiness of being a new bride. Because of my antics, neither did I.

"Don't be. I just feel like things are getting back to normal. I'm really sorry for what you went through. I don't understand it all but I know it wasn't you. It was someone else."

"I'm desperately trying to believe that myself but the alien was me and I remember everything she did." The milk begins to simmer and I pour it while Katie pours the coffee into the cups at the same time.

I lean against the bar and take a sip. "Oh this is good."

"Does it hurt to sit?" Katie asks shyly.

"Yeah. It's not as sore as it was. It's slowly healing. The stitches are to the point of itching, which my doctor says is a good thing.

"My God, Shelli. You've been through so much more than the rest of us. We were all sitting around feeling sorry for ourselves. I don't know what to say."

I hold the coffee cup to my mouth, click my teeth on the rim. I don't know what to say either.

"We felt betrayed—until you landed in ICU the first time. Then we were in shock. Zack was so strong. We all thought you would die but Zack never stopped pumping us up, reminding us how strong you were. After we had that terrible meeting, Zack investigated every angle. He even went to see Gregoire again. Zack is an extraordinary man, Shelli. I was so angry at you for letting yourself get so tangled up with the wrong people, even one I'm related to. I couldn't imagine that you would leave Zack for that scumbag." Katie pauses, runs her fingers through her hair to puff it out then takes hold of it near her scalp, squeezing so tightly that her knuckles turn white.

"It wasn't his fault. He only facilitated the inevitable."

She shrugs. "What I'm trying to say is that I'm happy about your diagnosis. I knew you wouldn't betray Zack in your right mind. I knew it." Tears begin to form in Katie's eyes.

"Hey, none of that. We've all cried too much already." I try to smile. "Thanks for supporting Zack through all this. I'm sorry it took me so long to get my head together before I called. I honestly thought you might hang up on me." I sip my coffee. "There's still a little paranoia and a profound sadness. But every minute seems more like old times. Seeing you is more than wonderful. This weekend when the three slobber sisters get together, now that will be marvelous."

"Can I ask you something personal?"

I raise an eyebrow. "Since when do you have to ask permission, silly? Ask away."

"Why didn't you run away? I mean why did you stay long enough to get beaten to a pulp?"

In a way, Katie seems to be taking the blame for all that's happened to me. She believes everything started at her wedding reception, Gregoire is her cousin, and, in her precious, innocent eyes, she can't believe that I begged for this beating. I explain all I think she can take. She accepts the alien theory but I worry that she'll never forgive herself for getting married in New Orleans.

"Fortunately, now, I know the difference between sex and love. My relationship with Zack is...good. He's having a little trouble with the depths of my infidelity." I pause, hoping Katie can handle the rest of what needs to be said. "I'm afraid that sex will never be as good as before, that I'll never have an orgasm again."

"Afraid that you won't have one or that it won't be as good?"

I wrap my arms around my chest. "Sometimes, I try to convince myself that what I need is love. I remember what you said the night Beka showed us our wedding gowns, something about love transcending sex, something about there being nothing like falling asleep in the arms of someone who loves you. I try to believe that love is going to be enough for me."

"There's nothing wrong with good, healthy sex between two people who love each other. You had it before."

"Yes but my mind gets so stressed over it." I'm afraid to say more. Ashamed. Embarrassed. I don't want her to know about last night, about faking enjoyment. The scene of

Gregoire fucking Rosalie in front of me flashes through my mind. I want to reach out, touch Rosalie's breasts. I'm being pulled apart. I crave the sex but I'm alcohol free. I am the alien. I shake my head, try to listen to Katie, try to focus on her positive words. She's trying to pull me out of the mire.

"You have to believe that you'll have it again. Take it slow. Everything isn't going to go back to the way it was before. Maybe it will be better now." Katie looks at her watch. "I know I don't have to thank you for being so candid. It helps to understand. I wish we could talk longer but I really have to be on time for my meeting. Let me hug you again." Katie wraps her warm arms around me and holds tight. "Everything's going to work out fine. You'll see." Pulling away slightly, she says, "I have to go to Atlanta tonight but I'll be back Friday. Can we get together then?"

My mind is muddled, foggy. "Of...course. It's best...right now, if you...come here."

"What happened, Shelli? Did I say something wrong?" Katie bites her lower lip. Her expression is horrifying me.

"No, I just have to tell you one more thing before you go." I take in a deep breath. "I have a dependency on alcohol. I'm an alcoholic."

Katie stares at me with such compassion. She reaches out for my hand. "That was difficult to say, wasn't it?"

"It's getting easier. It was extremely difficult to admit it to myself. I just admitted it for the first time yesterday."

"I'm so proud of you. You're right here." Katie taps her chest, over her heart. "See you Friday. We'll bring pizza."

As Katie drives away, I feel blessed. I try to hold on to the feeling. There are good pieces of me clamoring toward the surface of my reality. I don't think it's physician, heal thyself. It's physician, be healed by your husband, your parents, your friends. What will I say to Dr. Sloan tomorrow? Shall I tell him that I'm the alien and I still exist or tell him how a husband's caress, a lighted candle, a cup of half coffee, half steamed milk, and two gracious friends can heal a mind gone haywire?

As Katie disappears from view, the misty morning air slowly turns into a cloudburst. I let the rain cleanse me. Whatever this is—dare I call it God—leaves me with an awe-inspiring realization of wellbeing. I look to the sky in a gesture of thankfulness and I'm blinded by a sudden burst of lightning. I feel Naomi's blue drape engulf me and I am safe.

## 16

This morning, Dr. Sloan seems cautious over my progress. He tells me that my dichotomy of feelings is normal. He doesn't think my vision of Bourbon Street or my aversion to sex with Zack is something to worry about and he praises me for telling him. He thinks I'm expecting too much too fast. The medications have just begun to stabilize my psychosis. That gives me hope. "We'll continue your cognitive therapy until you learn to change and control your negative thoughts," he says. I want to believe him. He says that our sessions will continue twice a week until he is convinced that I can make it without professional help—"months to years." A long recovery depresses me. I try to block out a timeframe. One step at a time. One day at a time. I don't want to be sad.

I don't tell him of my ecstatic experiences for fear he'll think they were hallucinations. I have thoughts of Naomi's drape endlessly. It comes to me in different ways. Sometimes covering my entire body, much like a bridal veil, sometimes in sleep, to cover me in comfort. Other times the drape wraps itself around my head like the head dressing of my ancestors. Once it became a shroud for my burial. None of this draping accompanies fear or confusion as it is exquisite in its translucent brilliance. I interpret it as I do the clear ocean—my paradise. I am compelled to keep this experience to myself, for what reason I don't know, except that some higher power seems to be on my side in my battle for sanity. Is it the god of my father or am I escaping into a made-up religion as my salvation?

Early this evening I hear a soft knock on the door. I expect Zack any minute and presume that the knock is him needing my help to bring in the groceries. I'm surprised to see Zack's parents standing meekly and breathing heavily as if they have bad news. "Hello," I say, trying to sound cheerful. "Come in." I haven't seen them since the wedding. I suddenly wonder why Zack hasn't taken me to visit or even talked about them. It's almost as if I'd forgotten they existed. While I try to sort things out, Mom pulls me to her.

"We were so afraid," she says holding me so tightly I can feel a quivering in her muscles. "First, we couldn't believe—"

"My behavior?" I say breaking away but still both of us holding on to one another's arms.

"We were afraid that we'd lose you—like we lost Emma. We couldn't face that. Finally, we're blessed with another daughter then just as quickly as we...bond, well, you started to slip away."

"That girl who was slipping away, she wasn't me."

"We know that now. We came to apologize for turning our backs."

"You never turned from me, just from her—a girl who doesn't exist anymore. A girl I'm stamping out."

Finally, Zack's father speaks. He's been standing in the background twisting a package in his hands. "We're too self-centered. We've felt sorry for ourselves too long."

"What do you mean?" I say even though I know exactly what he's talking about. I want to call him *Dad* but I find that difficult even after all this time.

"Shelli, you're the only woman Zack ever cared about," he says handing the package to me, making eye contact with his wife as if he expects her to put the right words into his mouth. I ache for him in his uneasiness. "What I'm trying to say is that we've always been afraid that you would take Zack away from us. We probably didn't get to know you better on purpose. We're sorry for that now."

"You don't have—"

"Yes, I do." He takes in a deep breath and blows it out in almost a whistle. "Just before your wedding, we saw the real you. We accepted you and started loving you. We had a daughter again."

"It's true, dear." Mom pulls me closer. "But when you went away and ended up in ICU, we...doubted you."

"Everyone did. I'm sorry that I've disappointed everyone. I'm sorry that I disrupted everyone's lives."

"No, Shelli." Zack's father takes a step closer. "We understand now. Zack hung on to you, believed in you. He stayed in his old room at our house. We could hear him weeping and banging his fists against the wall. We'd lost one child to death, we thought we were losing Zack to this nightmare."

"We knew Zack couldn't live without you and we couldn't live without Zack. We were torn." Mom looks to her husband.

Suddenly I'm freezing. The stress causing my loss of reality was not only my nightmare—it was everyone's horror.

"Can we all sit down?" Mom nods toward the sofa.

"Yes, of course. I'm sorry." Feelings of confusion and shame fill me. Mom sits next to me. Zack's father sits in a recliner across from us. I lean back but Mom sits just on the edge. She turns slightly toward me with her hand on my knee.

"The last time we saw Emma was in ICU. We couldn't go into another ICU to see you. We ignored you out of selfish pity."

"We're not here to accuse you, Shelli." Zack's father's eyes mist up. "We're here to welcome you home. We love you. Please let us be your...parents again. We realize that we can't live without you just as much as Zack can't live without you."

"I am your daughter." My tears drip and my nose runs. I sniff. I don't have a tissue. "When I married Zack, I said the words of Ruth, 'your people shall be my people.' I meant it then. I mean it now. I need you to love me."

Zack's father comes to me and kneels before me. He takes my face in his hands. "It shall be done."

"Dad," I say pausing a moment, "and Mom, thank you for telling me everything. I love you all the more for it."

Zack bursts into the room balancing several grocery bags against his chest. "Well, well, what do we have here—an old-fashioned love-in?"

"That's exactly what it is," Dad says. "We dropped by to see if we could take you out to dinner." He stands to help with the grocery bags.

"Well, I beat you to it. You can eat with us. I stopped by The Fresh Market on my way home. There's more than enough for the four of us."

"Please stay," I beg. "I made a new dessert this afternoon."

"What did you make?" Mom asks. "Something chocolate?"

"Of course. I copied a recipe from *Gourmet* or *Bon Appetite* a few years back. It has lots of calories, more than I needed in the past. But I'm trying to gain weight."

"Umm, what is it?" The way Mom smiles at me, the acceptance in it, makes me feel like her daughter.

"Cappuccino Torte—it's chocolate, butter, cream, sugar, and...Zack? Did you find some chocolate-covered coffee beans?"

"Yes ma'am. I did." Zack pulls them from one of his shopping bags and holds them up in front of his smiling face.

"Sounds like dinner better be light," Mom says, eyes sparkling now. She seems to be right where she wants to be—one with her kids, her darling son and her darling new daughter who has returned from a nightmare.

Zack unpacks the rest of his shopping bag on to the coffee table. "Potato walnut salad, Greek salad, dolmades, a baguette, truffle mousse pâté, two kinds of cheese—one French, one Italian."

"Oh my. It doesn't look like we'll be eating light." Mom pats her stomach. "International cuisine."

"Well, as international as we can get in Chapel Hill." Zack gathers some of the food and places it on the bar behind us. "Are you ready to eat, Shell?" Zack stands behind the sofa, leans over my head to kiss me upside-down.

"I'm starving." I lean back and look up. He kisses me again.

"First, we want both of you to open the package." Mom scoots away. "Come, Zack. Sit between us.

A simple brown box tied with twine reveals a heart-shaped mosaic frame. The irregular pieces have been exquisitely mounted and the words L'chaim. are painted on one side. The heart encases a picture from our wedding—Zack and I are in the center with my parents to Zack's left and his parents to my right. There we are. The perfect family, all of us smiling into the future.

"Mom," Zack says unable to take his eyes off the frame. "You made this, didn't you? It's the broken pieces of the cup I crushed at our wedding."

"It is." I look from the frame to Mom's smiling face.

"If I do say so myself, the original was beautiful." Mom folds her hands on her lap. "I just couldn't throw the pieces away."

"Especially after what happened," Zack's father keeps his eyes glued to the frame. "I mean it seemed we were a broken family for a while but now, well, we've been put back together."

"To life." I say determined that this fairy tale wedding will have a happily ever after ending in spite of me.

Friday night, Katie and Sean breeze in loaded down with shopping bags.

"What's all this?" I ask.

"Here's the pizzas—three different kinds." Katie says as Sean hands them to Zack.

"Anyone interested in antipasto?" Zack asks on his way into the kitchen.

We answer, "Yes," in unison.

"Katie, do you want me to work on these pizzas?" Zack asks.

"No, I'll handle them," she says. "Go, sit, I'll be right there."

"What can I get everyone to drink? Wine, beer, iced tea, soft drinks? I think there's some juice too." Zack moves aside to let Katie deal with the pizzas.

"Do you have ginger ale?" Katie asks.

Zack looks into the fridge. "Sure do."

"Ginger ale for me then." Katie says without looking up.

"Me too. Ginger ale." I feel like the party-pooper. Poor, sweet Katie. She'll probably never drink champagne or a beer in front of me again.

When Zack tastes the pizza, he licks his lips. "This pizza is delicious, Katie. How did you have time to make it?"

Katie smiles and plays along. "When I got home from the airport, I just threw it together."

"Shut up," I say, laughing. "Come on. Tell the truth, Susie Homemaker."

"Well, glory be, Rhett, they don't believe I can cook." Katie speaks in a coy, southern accent. "I actually flew in at two this very afternoon."

"Scarlet." Sean smiles. "Next you'll be telling them, just like Prissy, that you don't know about birthin' babies."

"Babies?" My eyes are wide with expectation. "Babies? Is there something you want to tell us, Katie?"

Katie answers without losing the southern accent. "I'll answer the first question first. I lied about the pizza. When I was in Atlanta previously, I scouted out the sweetest little bakery, not two blocks from the Hotel Magnolia. They just happen to carry these little delicacies. And you did, did you not, see me put them into your very own oven? So, that proves that Scarlet can indeed cook. As for the second question, I do not, ma'am, know anything about birthing babies but I do know when one is with child and I am."

"I thought you didn't want a beer because of me. You're pregnant! Congratulations. When did you find out?"

"Today. Sean met me at the gynecologist on my way home from the airport." Katie looks down at her hands. Her cheeks flush.

"We heard her heartbeat." Sean puts an arm around Katie. They lean their heads together. "I just can't tell you what a fabulous feeling that is."

"*Her* heartbeat?" I'm puzzled.

"Yes." Sean's grin is wide. "We're sure of it. Besides, we just want one child. We decided she should be a girl, so we did all the things people have to do to get a girl. We found pages of instructions on the net."

"Like what?" Zack laughs.

"Well, I didn't tie my right testicle off," Sean says.

"What does that have to do with it?" Zack looks at me.

"The ancient Greeks believed that sperm from the left testicle produced females," Sean says, "and the right produced males. Hell, some French noblemen had their left nuts cut off completely to ensure they had male heirs."

"Katie." I squeal. "What did you do? Tell us, we may need to know someday."

"All I'm going to say is her name is Laura Katherine." Katie puffs out her chest.

"Come here, let me feel your belly," I say.

Katie stands next to me. I feel a slight bump on her otherwise tight belly. "Ahh, nice. Did you get pregnant on your honeymoon?" I can't conceal my delight.

"The time was right for a girl, so we went for it," Katie says, really flushed now.

"The right time wouldn't have come around again for several months," Sean explains. "So, we got to it a little earlier than the honeymoon."

"Sean." Katie glares. "We've been married nine weeks, five days. The midwife's little dial showed that I was nine weeks and three days pregnant."

"Congratulations, man." Zack salutes Sean, "You got her pregnant on your honeymoon. But was the time still right? Maybe two days was too late. You might have a boy."

"The window was a week. We wanted to make certain we gave it a good shot." Sean turns to Katie. "Don't let Zack upset you, Scarlet. Our baby is a girl. A little Irish-American, just like her mama."

"So how are two Catholics going to have just one baby?" Zack jests.

"As soon as we know that the baby is healthy, we're both going to turn into sports models." Sean laughs and we all laugh with him.

"Catholic sports models?" Zack screws up his face in teasing disbelief.

"Yeah. Seriously," Katie says, "we just want one child, while we're young. She'll be out of high school by the time we're forty-three when most people still have babies in diapers. Shelli, you were almost an only child so you probably don't understand what it's like to have sisters and brothers. We want Laura to have a good life. She'll have to get her siblings from you and Beka."

While Katie speaks, I realize that I haven't had a period since...when? Panic crashes down on our little reunion party. Let me think? When? I can't remember. My last cycle was...before we got married? My mind counts the weeks. Thirteen. No. I am *not* pregnant. Not now. Please, God, not now. Birth control pills? I stopped taking them when I went to New Orleans the first time. Please, God, no. I can't be pregnant by Gregoire or Jonathan. I can't be.

"Shelli? Are you alright?" Zack is at my side, rubbing my back.

"I didn't get a nap today. I'm feeling tired, sorry."

"Why don't you crash, Shelli?" Katie says. "I need extra sleep lately. I have an early meeting in the morning to hopefully settle with the Atlanta clients. Come on, I'll help you to bed. The boys have pizza and beer left."

While I slip into my gown, Katie brews some tea for my sitz bath. When it's ready, Katie leads me to it and then sits on the edge of the bathtub. She leans her head against my shoulder. "I'm so proud of you. I can't wait for Beka. Next week is going to be so awesome."

"I know." My mind seems so far away. My terror returns. What about my triumphant battle? Being pregnant right now would be…I can't bear to think what it would do to Zack, what it would do to *us*.

Katie and I sit in silence for what seems an eternity. She, probably dreaming of a baby in her arms while I plan an abortion. Until this very instant, I didn't believe abortion was for me under any circumstance but then I never imagined being in a situation like this where an alien's baby would ruin my relationship with Zack, with my parents, his parents—with everyone.

Katie interrupts my nightmarish musing. "Since Beka probably won't be here until late Sunday night, I'll see you both Monday morning. Hopefully, I can arrange to take Monday off. That is if I can finish this project tomorrow. Besides, it will give you time to spend with Beka alone. You both need that. Just call me when you wake up. I'll come by then."

"That's sweet of you."

"Oh that reminds me, I thought of a gift for Beka, for making our gowns."

"Good. What?" I try to be optimistic but my emotions are about to betray me.

"Well, I was thinking about how different our weddings were, yet the colors we chose match so well."

"What do you mean?"

"I was thinking about us making her a quilt. She gave me scraps from all the gowns. There's enough for a quilt. All those luxurious fabrics together will be striking. She won't be able to refuse a personal gift like that, will she?"

"No, she won't. But you know I can't quilt."

"You won't have to do the quilting—my new machine can do that part." Katie smiles. "There's a simple yet elegant pattern called *Regalia*. It's just four-inch squares sewn on an angle. All you'll have to do is help cut the squares and sew them together."

"If you say so." I try to mirror Katie's excitement but my worries overcome me. "I'm ready for bed now." I stand to empty the sitz bath. "Katie?"

"Yes?"

"How about lighting a candle for me at church."

Katie follows me into the bedroom and helps me into bed. She pulls the covers over my quivering body. "I always light one for you, you know that."

"Will you light one for Zack?"

Katie kneels beside me. "Something's wrong. You were fine a moment ago. What is it?"

"Nothing. Everything. I'm so confused right now."

"About what?" Katie's eyes have gone from glittering green to subdued gray as she stares into mine.

I roll over with my back to her. "I just need some sleep. Call me in the morning, okay?"

"No. It's not okay. What just happened, Shelli? Tell me?"

Katie rests her hand on my shoulder. She rolls me to face her.

"Thirty minutes ago you had the world by the tail," she says with a look of kindness mixed with exasperation. "Now you're pouting, depressed. Did I say something wrong?"

My mind fills with fear. I can't hold back the flood of tears.

"I'm sorry. I didn't mean to badger you. I want to understand."

"It's about your baby." I sit up, grab a tissue from the box on the table next to the bed. "I can't remember when my last period was. I can't remember having a period since before my wedding. I could be pregnant too." A zillion scenarios flash through my mind. "Do you get what I'm saying? I won't even know who the father is, there were so many men."

"Shelli, no." Katie moves to sit on the side of the bed beside me.

"I can't be pregnant. I can't be."

Katie's rocking me now but I feel no comfort, just terror. "Hush, now," she says. "Take a deep breath. Blow it out real slow, real slow."

I try but all I can do is tremble. Katie holds me tighter.

"Wouldn't the hospital have done a pregnancy test? If it was positive they would have told you long ago."

"They told me that my blood alcohol level was sky high but my drug screen was negative. No one said anything about a pregnancy test."

"You're probably not pregnant. If you are we'll all help you deal with it. No one is going to let you go through whatever you have to go through alone."

"I'm so afraid."

"So am I." Katie kisses my hair like I'm a baby and for a millisecond I feel protected.

"I don't want to ruin everyone's life."

"We love you too much to let that happen." Katie helps me lie back. "Do you want me to get Zack?"

Panic hits me hard. "I can't tell Zack. I can't hurt him anymore. I can't—" I grab Katie's knee. She takes my hand in both of hers.

"Zack will understand. He'll want to help you as much as I do. Honestly."

"Why am I so afraid?"

Katie hesitates, looks away. She squeezes my hand tighter. When she gathers her thoughts, she looks back. "Maybe because you're rushing things. Healing takes time, Shelli—we have a lot of time ahead of us."

"Yeah. Time." I bite my upper lip until I bite off a tiny piece of skin. "You better get some sleep."

Katie kisses my cheek then stands to leave. "I'll send Zack in. Sean and I can clean up the kitchen. Good night, my slobber sister. I'll call you in the morning."

My heart pounds in my throat. I stare at the ceiling, letting the humming of crickets and tree frogs outside the window mesmerize me and stop my mind from derailing. Zack comes to bed and snuggles close.

"There's something big, Zack. I'm afraid. Hold me tight."

"What is it, baby? Is it Katie's pregnancy?"

With my face burrowed against Zack's neck, I try to gather enough courage to express my fear. Finally, I let out a long breath. "When Katie said how long she'd been pregnant, I realized that I haven't had a period in weeks. If I was pregnant with your child, I could deal with it. What if I'm pregnant with someone else's—"

"Don't say it, Shelli."

"I have to say it." I pull away to face Zack. "I don't want to have Gregoire's or Jonathan's baby or anyone else's for that matter. I only want your baby."

Zack sighs heavily. "Wait a minute. I'm sure that the first time you were in ICU the doctors did a pregnancy test and it was negative. They probably did one the second time too. Besides, you've lost, what, twenty pounds? Maybe that's why you haven't had a period. Stress and weight loss. Am I right?"

"I pray that you are but what if you're not?"

"Do you want me to get a pregnancy test kit and prove it to you?"

"No. I can't bear to know right now. "If there's a baby in there it's full of alcohol. It will be born deformed—"

"Stop." Zack puts his hand to my mouth. "Don't worry until there's something to worry about. First thing tomorrow morning we'll get a pregnancy test. It'll be negative. Believe me."

I pull at my hair. "What if, just what if it's not?"

"Then we'll deal with it together. Remember we're in this together."

Zack clings to me. I feel numb, lifeless, as if I'm sinking, disappearing, disintegrating. What if this poison is growing inside of me? What if I produce another alien? What will become of me if I'm carrying a child created by my own immorality?

The morning sun causes me to turn away from the window. Zack's arm rests on my hip. When I roll to face him, his smile welcomes me.

"Good morning, beautiful." He moves closer to kiss me.

I click my tongue. "I made it through the night."

"Yes, you did."

"It's because you held me." I snuggle closer.

"It's because you let me hold you."

"Can we pick up a few pregnancy test kits now? I'm not dealing well with this great big question mark hanging over my head. If I *am* pregnant, we need to talk about our options before Beka gets here. I don't want anything to get in the way of our reunion."

"Why don't you hop in the shower while I run to the drug store and Starbuck's."

"Okay. Get a few kits, different brands, just to be sure."

"My silly." Zack ruffles my hair.

Hot water washes over me as I stand in the shower trying to force my anxiety down the drain. I try to control my breathing, try to imagine the ocean waves rocking me in comfort. I wonder why I wanted to run from my fears last night, run from all that's good in another wake of madness. The haunting fear of what could mar my happiness—a child severely cursed with Fetal Alcohol Syndrome to remind us daily of my escapades in New Orleans. My lack of strength frightens me. Although Zack is here trying to save me, I feel alone in my own private dark night. What if I can't be saved? I imagine gin burning my throat and ripening my perverse sexuality. I am horror-struck. I have to stand in this water until Zack comes home. When will I be able to trust myself?

Zack peeks into the shower. "Look what I have for you—hot coffee, cinnamon scones, and four pregnancy kits. Come, let me dry you off."

I feel my heart splinter. Will Zack love me as much if this baby I carry isn't his? I'm praying now, sucking back tears while Zack wraps one towel around me and dries my hair with another. This compassion is more than I deserve. *Please, God, please*, I beg. I turn to Zack. "I hope you'll love me this much in a few minutes." I tear into the first of the boxes. "Let's get it over with."

Zack smiles but I see fear in his eyes. Not fear that I'll be pregnant but fear of my reaction to it. He's afraid that I'll not be as strong as we both hope I will be.

I sit on the toilet while Zack stands ready with the four wicks. I take them from him one by one and hold my breath. Negative. Negative. Negative. Negative. Zack holds me. Our tears mingle. "Thank God." I say. When we're able to part, Zack removes the towel from around my body and dresses me in a terry cloth robe. He stands behind me, his arms encompass my waist before coming to rest on my pelvis. "Someday," he says, "we'll cry with joy when the tests turn out positive. Someday our love will make handsome sons and beautiful daughters who will put smiles on our faces. Come on. Our coffee is getting cold."

The dreary weather all weekend has increased my fear of relapsing. I am cold despite pulling a wool sweater over my flannel PJs. I snuggle under a down comforter and try to focus on Beka's visit. Zack trusted me enough to leave me alone this morning to play golf with a buddy from work. Fortunately, Mama and Zack's mother came by earlier. We made hot cocoa from scratch. We talked but I couldn't bring myself to tell them about this latest episode in my dramatic life, though I longed to. I guess I'm protecting them. We talked of happy things—Katie's baby, Beka's visit, and even the burning of the gin celebration. They smiled the way proud mothers do, and I decided that I never want either of them to cry over me again.

"Honey, I'm home." Zack calls from the front door. "Yumm, something smells good."

"Believe it or not, I'm cooking dinner." I hurry to greet him.

"It smells like potato blintzes, my favorite." He looks over my shoulder, hugging me before smothering me with kisses.

"Look here," I say as I remove the lid from a saucepan on the stove. "Homemade applesauce."

"Now you're talking. You must want something special from me." Zack teases my ear with his tongue.

I don't tell him that I'm cooking mainly to keep my mind occupied while I'm alone. Instead, I force my words. "You must have something you want to give me before Beka gets here."

Tears brim his eyes. "I love you, Shelli. I'm so proud of you." He pulls me tighter into his embrace but instead of feeling at peace, like I thought I would when he got home, I feel as if he's surprised I'm still here.

"How was your golf game?"

"Other than missing you, and just about every putt on the course, it was fine."

As he continues telling me about his game, I nod and smile and giggle but my mind is someplace else. Will anyone ever trust me again?

After we clean up the kitchen, Zack leads me to the bedroom. It's seven-thirty. Beka won't arrive for another three or four hours. I let Zack hold me but refuse his romantic advances, feigning exhaustion, which is only partially true. Almost immediately, I fall asleep in Zack's arms. As I drift off, I try to remember what my life once was.

The phone awakens me. I hear Zack talking in the living room. I squint at the clock—two a.m. Beka. I jump from the bed as Zack enters the bedroom, pale, shaking, the phone pressed to his ear.

"What is it?" I feel hot tears because of the way he's looking at me. "Please tell me."

## 17

"What is it?" I pace the floor, listening to Zack mumble into the phone, "Uh-huh…yes…uh-huh." His face is ashen, his hands tremble.

As he lowers his phone, he avoids my eyes. "It's Beka. I'm so sorry, Shelli."

"What? What about her? What about Beka?" I'm trembling now also.

"That was Beka's mom on the phone. There's been an accident. It's all this rain."

"Tell me, Zack, tell me she's alive." Zack is holding me now.

"She's alive, but—"

"But what?"

"When she exited I-40, she was stopped at the light on Farrington Road. The car behind her hydroplaned, pushing her into the intersection. Then she was broadsided by a car coming through on Highway 54. It took the Fire Department over an hour to get her out of the car. She's in surgery right now at UNC. Get dressed and we'll go check things out."

My knees buckle under me. I sit on the end of the bed too shocked to cry, too shocked to think.

"Come on, honey," Zack says. I feel his strength. He pulls a pair of black silk pajama bottoms from my lingerie drawer. "Can you wear these?"

"Yes." I exchange the flannel bottoms for the black ones. I'm still wearing my wool sweater over my pajama top. I'm shivering cold again. I slip into a pair of black clogs while Zack covers me with my waterproof parka before we head for the car. "Did Mrs. Schultzberg know why Beka's in surgery?"

"Yeah."

"Don't keep anything from me, please," I beg as I fasten my seat belt.

Zack almost stutters. "A head injury, some broken bones, internal bleeding."

"Which bones?" I'm panicking now.

"Skull, ribs, pelvis…neck."

"Neck? Oh my God, no." I shriek. "No." I think of Ben Lowenstein's blue still body at the bottom of the town pool. I think of his funeral. I think of Christopher Reeve's nine years of life on a ventilator. He thought he'd walk again but he's dead. "Is she paralyzed?"

"They don't know for sure. She was unconscious at the scene. Probably doesn't know what hit her." Zack squeezes my hand. "It might not be as bad as we think. You have to be strong for her. She's going to need you when she wakes up."

Dazed, I stare into the blinding rain. It's all my fault. She was coming to see me. She was just a few blocks away. What a goddammed, fucking disaster I've made of our lives.

At the emergency department, we're directed to a surgery waiting room. Katie and Sean sit comforting Mrs. Schultzberg. There are other people here. People I don't recognize.

When Katie sees us, she runs to me. "Why, Shelli, why are the three of us together *again* for the wrong reasons? What's gone wrong with our lives? Just when everything is good again, just when we finally got you back, now this. Why?"

"Is there any news on Beka?" Zack asks.

"She's still in surgery. That's all we know." Mrs. Schultzberg speaks without looking up.

Zack looks at his watch. "When was the last time you got an update?"

"Nearly an hour ago," Katie says, staring at the swinging doors into the surgical suite.

"Shelli." Mrs. Schultzberg looks straight at me with eyes red as fire. There are tear stains on her shirt. "Can you call your father? He can find out more. Can't he?"

I nod. She knows it's my fault. She's already blaming me.

"Do you want me to call him?" Zack looks to me for permission.

I nod again, clenching my jaw and fists, trying to control my breathing.

"Let me step outside. Cell phones aren't allowed in here. I'll be right back."

Sean leads me to a row of seats adjacent to Beka's mom. Katie buries her face in Sean's chest while I sit straight feeling a sharp pain from the wounds on my bottom, the wounds that caused all this grief, the wounds that caused Beka's accident, the wounds that will come to separate the slobber sisters forever.

"Shelli's parents are on their way," Zack says before sitting next to me. He pulls me to him. "How are you holding up?"

I drop my head. We all sit in silence until my parents arrive.

Daddy speaks briefly with Beka's mom while Mama tries to comfort me. She holds my face in her hands as Daddy disappears behind the doors that have DO NOT ENTER written on them in big red letters. Mama curls her hands around mine and for the first time tonight, I feel warmth. She knows what I know, that all this is my fault, that I am the reason these people are here tonight. I hear everyone's hearts shatter into thousands of pieces. I don't look up.

It seems like forever before Daddy reappears through the swinging doors. I look to him with hopeful expectations.

"She's in critical condition. Both her spleen and one kidney were ruptured. Both have been removed. She's receiving blood transfusions now. Her pelvis is fractured but it's in alignment so shouldn't cause her any problems. She has a small skull fracture and a few broken ribs…minor complications." He stops, looks at me while he takes a handkerchief from his back pocket. He wipes his forehead before continuing. "Four vertebrae are fractured and compressing the spinal cord. There's a fair amount of swelling. The doctors are doing everything possible under the circumstances."

"Will she be paralyzed?" A man sitting next to Beka's mom has the gall to ask.

"I don't know. They've administered steroids to relieve the swelling. There's much intricate, tedious work to be done before they'll know if the spinal cord has been damaged to the point of paralysis. It may take—"

A voice blares from an overhead speaker, "Code blue, OR three. Code blue, OR three."

"Is Beka in OR three?" I yell because I see the panic on Daddy's face. I break away from Mama. I taste gin. I need gin. I need to get out of here. I need out of here forever. "Give me the car keys." I reach for Zack's pocket. Just as my hand touches his trousers, he grabs the keys, holds them behind his back. "Give them to me."

"Why, Shell? Where are you going?"

"I'm poison. Can't you see? I've killed Beka. This is all my fault. Give me the keys, now." I fight with Zack, trying to get the keys. I feel Daddy's grip on my arm, hear Mama's soft cry. "See what I've done? See? If Beka doesn't die, she'll be just like Ben Lowenstein. She'll rot away because of me."

"We don't know that," Daddy says, still holding tightly to my arm.

"Yes we do. We know. Why can't you tell the truth? Why are you giving us false hope? Beka won't make it out of the OR. She'll die and be all the better for it. Just blame it on me. Now, give me the damn keys, Zack. Give me the damn fuckin' keys." I beat his chest with my free arm. I cry out, struggling as Zack and Daddy wrestle me to the floor. "Give me a drink. I'm a fucking alcoholic. I need a fucking drink. Let me go. Give me the damn fucking keys." I wrestle with the men in my life as I'm lifted onto a gurney and swept away through the swinging doors. My head bumps metal rails as I thrash from side-to-side. Bright lights constrict my vision. I feel a needle penetrate my thigh, my struggling stops, the world turns black.

I awake to the stark white, stiff sheets of a hospital bed. It's daylight, maybe mid-morning. My head aches so badly that I have difficulty opening my eyes. Zack's head rests on my thigh, his body slumped forward from a straight-backed chair. I can tell by his breathing that he's sleeping. Mama is asleep in a reclining chair on the other side of the bed. Her hand loosely holds my fingers below an IV in my wrist. When I squeeze it, she opens her eyes and smiles.

"Good morning, darling." Although she is smiling, I see weary, worried eyes.

My eyes dart from Mama to Zack. "Where am I?"

Zack sits up, shakes his head then stands. He leans to kiss my forehead. "You had a little relapse, honey." His voice is as morose as a mortician.

At once, I remember. "Beka." I cry out, covering my face with my hands.

"Beka's doing well so far," Zack says.

"Your father says she's a miracle." Mama reaches through the rail to pull my hands away from my face.

"She's not paralyzed?"

Mama exchanges glances with Zack.

"Please tell me she's not paralyzed." I hold Mama's hand, as my eyes pierce the blank stare on Zack's face.

"We don't know yet." He hangs his head. "It may take days before the swelling goes down."

"The doctors don't want her to wake up until the swelling is gone." Mama nods. "Her spinal cord is flattened, not severed."

"So, there's hope." I close my eyes.

Zack kisses my eyelids. "That's my positive girl."

"I do feel different today. Better, except for this headache. My mind is clear, my thoughts coherent." I look to Zack then to Mama. "What did they give me?"

"Sedatives, something for anxiety." Zack squeezes my hand.

"So, I'm not as well as I thought."

"You've only seen the psychiatrist twice," Zack reminds me gently. "Remember when Stan first spoke with your father? He said the minimum you could expect is a three-month recovery. You've just been under treatment less than a week."

"I was actually almost myself again." I squint, feeling the muscles of my eyelids twitch. I let the experiences of the past few days catch up with me while Mama and Zack look at me with sad, blank faces.

"You can talk about it. It's not good to keep things tied up inside." Mama squeezes my hand. "You're a strong woman but you're as fragile as Beka right now."

"Oh Beka." The tears come now. "We shouldn't be worrying about me. Beka's life is hanging by a thread. What kind of friend am I? We should all be at Beka's side, not here in this, this, where am I? A medical hospital or a... God. I'm in the psych ward, aren't I?"

"A minor setback." Zack pats my hand. "The news of Beka's accident was—"

"I don't want to land in a hospital bed every time my perfect little world goes off-kilter. I wanted a drink. Had I been here alone last night, I would have drowned my guilt in a couple bottles of gin then you'd be rid of me and my ridiculous behavior forever."

"That's enough, Shelli." Zack's voice rings with impatience.

"No, it's not enough. I'll never be me again. For the rest of my life, I'll have to rely on medication. A few days without it and I'll be right back to that little slut that tried to ruin your lives."

"That's not true. Now hush, listen to me." Zack's eyes are dull, listless. He's crumpled. Deep lines cross his forehead. "You'll just need the medicine until you're cured. You're so close, baby. So close."

I close my eyes again, realizing that Zack is right. I'm not cured. This psychosis lays hidden under all these fancy drugs, ready to lash out as soon as I let my defenses down. I force a smile through my tears, reach out to Zack and Mama. They both cling to me. I feel acceptance. Maybe I can beat this demon that has slithered its way into the depths of my consciousness. I take in a breath, hold it then let it out quickly. "I don't need to apologize for last night, do I?"

"Good work." Zack smiles at me. "What did I tell you? Three months max."

"I wish I was so optimistic."

Mama shakes her head. "You've always had a thing for instant gratification."

"Speaking of instant gratification, when can I get out of here?"

"Probably late this afternoon. Dr. Sloan wants to see you later this morning." Zack winks.

"What about Katie and Sean and Mrs. Schultzberg? I'm embarrassed to have to see them again."

"Don't worry about them. Your father explained everything. They understand," Mama says. "Katie and Sean are right outside. They slept in the waiting room last night, refused to leave you or Beka even though neither of you can have visitors except family."

"You all slept in chairs last night, didn't you?" I blow air slowly through pursed lips. "This is the last thing I want to do—hurt the people I love best."

"We know." Zack brushes my hair away from my eyes with his fingers.

"Where's Daddy?"

"He's checking on Beka." Mama squeezes my hand intermittently.

"I know in my head that the accident wasn't my fault but not in my heart."

"Maybe there's a reason for it you don't know," Mama says.

"Like what? Like what kind of reason is there for someone to be paralyzed?"

"The two of you grew up together, did everything together, graduated kindergarten, junior high, senior high, even college together." Mama leans forward. "Maybe God has a plan. Maybe you two should take care of each other, heal together."

"And *walk* out of here with *clear* minds," I say.

"There, you see—from your lips to God's ears."

"Thanks, Mama. Thanks for believing in me."

"Don't forget about Katie." Mama smiles.

"I remember when we were little, you said, 'One day you'll need each other even more than you need me?' Today's that day, isn't it?"

"Yes, darling. Today's the day." She squeezes my hand.

Daddy peeks in the door. "Well, well, well, my little shayneleh is awake."

"How's Beka?" I ask.

"Stable but serious. She's no longer critical. In a few days we'll know just how well she'll do. Things are more hopeful today."

I hold my arms wide, tears overflow. "I need a hug from you. When will all this end?"

Daddy hugs me, looks at me without speaking for a moment as if he's been asked one of those impossible questions by a patient of his. He takes in a breath and speaks softly, "This is life, Shelli. For twenty-five years your life has been charmed. Nothing that's happened these past couple months is unusual. People have mental and physical breakdowns every day, children die, car accidents happen. You've been immune to this kind of suffering all your life."

I pull away. "In other words, buck up."

Zack laughs. I see the tear he brushes away.

"Come, Sharon, let's go home," Daddy says, "and leave these love birds alone." He kisses the top of my head the way he's done for as long as I can remember. Even though he ritualistically gave me to Zack at our wedding, I'll always be his little girl. The thought comforts me.

Zack's gentle touch awakens me from my nap when Dr. Sloan enters the room.

My eyes, still heavy from sedation and guilt, open slowly. I try focusing on my psychiatrist. His eyes pierce mine. Have I let him down too?

"Good afternoon. Feeling better today?"

"Yes and no." I try to clear my head of the fog of medicines running through my IV. "I'm sorry. Dr. Sloan, this is my husband, Zack."

"We met last night while you were sleeping," the doctor says. He sits in the chair vacated by Mama.

"The psychosis is still with me."

Dr. Sloan reinforces what Zack, Mama, and Daddy have already told me. He says it will take time to regain my coping skills or learn new ones. I smile remembering Mama's diagnosis of instant gratification. He knows about my heavy load of guilt.

"I more fully understand your reaction to Beka's situation after learning about Ben and the life goal you've chosen because of him. Beka chose to visit you. How many times has she made that drive and arrived safely? Think more on this, what if, just what if Beka had decided to leave one minute earlier or one minute later. The accident probably wouldn't have happened. What if she had stopped for coffee or pulled into a rest stop for a half-hour? What if the car behind her hadn't hydroplaned? Many things could have been to blame—Beka herself, the rain, the other drivers, the types of cars they were driving or the speed each was traveling. There's no way you could have manipulated time and space to cause the sequence of events that led up to the impact."

I stop to think, clear my head. Dr. Sloan is partially right. "Not Beka. It's not Beka's fault. The rain is or maybe the car that hydroplaned." I'm treading water, lost in Zack's worried eyes. "There's always a what if, isn't there? Still, there'll be more stressors with Beka. Am I going to jump from a plane without a parachute every time my world falls apart? I want to be strong. I don't feel strong."

"Do you know what caused this latest outbreak?" the doctor asks.

I want to say guilt but I look to my lap. Was it my guilt or my lack of trust or maybe that I don't really accept my diagnosis? Maybe I don't think I can be cured, maybe Dr. Sloan is the wrong doctor. I don't trust Dr. Sloan—he sees my weaknesses. He'll betray me. My hands turn cold.

"Shell?" Zack grabs my hand. "What's wrong? What are you thinking?"

"Too many things. Too many."

"Can you tell me?" the doctor asks.

"I'm afraid to tell you what I'm thinking. My mind is jumbled." I look to Zack for support then back to the doctor. "I'm afraid everyone will get sick and tired of me, I'm afraid that everyone will...leave me, even you. I've let everyone down even though they've forgiven me."

"Admitting that you feel weak and afraid is another step in the right direction." Dr. Sloan smiles. It's the first time I've seen him smile. "The therapy will change you, slowly. You're on a steady path, regardless of this setback."

I try to let the doctor's words sink in. Until Naomi died, nothing ever really affected me enough to cause stress. Now, I don't know how to handle these things I have no experience with. My mind feels less jumbled. I realize that I need to share everything with Dr. Sloan, so I do. I tell him about my missed periods, the pregnancy scare, my ecstatic experience. I tell him about Naomi's translucent drape.

To my amazement, Dr. Sloan just nods then suggests that I join a gym or go to a spa, get a massage, a pedicure. He encourages me to take Mama, Katie, or even Zack along. I'm sure Zack could use a regular massage. But most of all, he advised me to give myself a break, then a reward.

"So, when can I get out of here?" I ask, feeling positive now and anxious to move on with my life.

"We'll stop your IV and restart your oral medications. Eat some lunch. If you feel well enough this afternoon, you can go home before dinner."

"I'll try not to have another setback before my next appointment." I joke.

"This is a minor setback. You've taken six steps forward and only one back." Dr. Sloan shakes my hand with compassion.

Maybe Mama is right. God's plan. Beka and me, fragile together, Katie too—her pregnancy overshadowed by my transmutation along with Beka's fight for life. I try to hold on. Once I was a spring breeze—soft, shimmering, serene. Now, I am a hurricane smashing my waves against the shore, leaving a path of destruction in my wake. I'm exhausted now. My eyelids are heavy.

## 18

Today marks the end of my second week in therapy. I remained hospitalized for longer than expected—four days. My *minor* setback turned into a major one. Only heavy sedation saved me that first day. Whenever the sedation was weaned, my terror, guilt, and sadness returned with such a vengeance that I had to be sedated once again with an IV antipsychotic. Late on the third day, the antidepressant finally took hold. I'm determined to never step back again—even if Beka should die. When she awakens from her drug-induced coma the doctors expect her to regain mobility. So, I sit and wait, and pray just as vehemently for Beka as the other 950 patients here are praying for themselves—that they will walk out of here alive. I emphasize *walk* in my prayer. Beka's accident was one week ago today. Her vital signs and electrolytes are stable. The doctors plan to wean her from the drug-induced coma in the next couple days. The two of us are neck-and-neck with our recovery—just as Mama predicted.

This morning, Dr. Sloan is impressed, yet cautious, over my progress. "Don't be surprised," he says, "if you should suddenly relapse back into depression or sorrow." No matter what he says, I feel positive and invigorated. I'm in control now. I know I am. I haven't experienced negative desires. I question the long recovery that Dr. Sloan predicts. My progress just this week has been rapid and already I've taken giant steps.

Katie and I now have permission to visit Beka. We enter the Neuro ICU with trepidation, each step an effort, every breath a struggle. Daddy warned us of Beka's hideous appearance but neither of us is prepared for this terrifying crypt. We clasp hands as we pass four glass-enclosed cubbyholes filled with so much machinery and flashing monitors that we can't see the patient inside.

Katie hesitates more than I do. I squeeze her hand as much for moral support for myself as for her. At least I'd seen an ICU before—both as a medical student and a patient but this one is different. This ICU holds our hearts.

From the door, Beka's stone-still profile reminds me of King Tut reclining in his Egyptian tomb. Beka's proud chin points to the sky but instead of King Tut's wide-eyed stare into eternity, Beka's eyes are taped shut. Her head is bald. Titanium pins, drilled into her skull, connect to a body harness that stabilizes her spine. A neatly folded, white sheet drapes her from armpits to knees. Foam rubber rolls hold her extremities in alignment. Dried blood and iodine stain the side of her head where the pins have been placed. The tape securing the ventilator tube pulls her mouth into a grotesque half-open position. Blood-tinged saliva has pooled in her mouth and is dripping down her cheek into her ears. The only movement is the rise and fall of her chest with each cycle of the ventilator.

Katie sits rigid in the chair beside the head of the bed, while I stand stroking Beka's arm. We look at each other, horrified. Katie whispers words of encouragement while I am dumfounded, unable to utter a word.

"Can she hear us?" Katie asks a nurse who introduces herself as Beka's caretaker.

"Probably," the nurse answers. "She's heavily sedated but I think she'll recognize your voice."

"Beka," Katie whispers, "it's me and Shelli. We're here…waiting for you. You're so strong. Everything's going to be fine, you'll see."

My throat is so clogged with tears that I can't speak. I don't want Beka to hear me cry. I squeeze Beka's hand. Katie gently covers our hands with hers. The nurse hands us a box of tissues then tells us our five minutes are up. Katie and I look at each other as we turn to leave. I wonder if anything can be worse than this.

My second visit with Beka isn't quite the shock that it was yesterday. I'm alone with Beka this morning. Katie will visit after work. I've decided to talk for my entire five minutes.

"Good morning, Sleeping Beauty. Are you dreaming of a handsome prince coming to kiss you awake?" I speak just above a whisper. "Think positive thoughts—like you always do. We need to talk, you know. So much has happened. I want to know everything about the new man in your life." While I ramble on, I imagine the swelling around Beka's spinal cord going down like flood waters receding. I imagine the day, very soon, when Beka will walk out of this revolting, antiseptic, horrific room.

The phone awakens me at five-thirty a.m. My heart thumps painfully. News at this hour can only be bad. I let the phone ring one more time before gathering the courage to answer. Daddy tells me that the doctors were able to wean Beka's sedation and ventilator settings. She's breathing without assistance. They will let her wake up from the drug-induced coma later this morning. If everything goes as planned, she'll be extubated this evening.

Because she can breathe, there's every reason to believe she won't be permanently paralyzed. Soon she'll feel tingling sensations in her hands and feet and this nightmare will be over. As I set the phone down, I sigh aloud.

"Who was that," Zack asks without opening an eye.

I tell him this exciting news and scoot down so we're face-to-face. "I can't wait to see her today." For a moment, the scary pounding changes to anticipation.

"Stop talking." Zack covers my lips with his mouth. My heart slows as I melt into him. I feel an honest, desperate desire to share my physical self with this perfect man. Beka and I are making progress. Zack's kisses are so passionate that they excite me. He presses against my thigh, gyrating and thrusting his hips until he moans in apparent euphoria.

"I love you, Zack. Soon, I'll be healed…then we can do this right."

He pulls me closer, as much to comfort me, I think, as to console himself while he waits for me to heal. It feels right to linger here in Zack's arms. This is where I belong.

Beka came off the ventilator two days ago. Today she's in a private room in the step-down unit from Neuro ICU. Since I can stay for several hours a day now, the physical therapist taught me how to exercise Beka's muscles so they won't atrophy. When Katie arrived after work, I taught her what the therapist taught me. Beka doesn't acknowledge our touch, and we don't see any spontaneous movement below her shoulders. The doctors think that the swelling has subsided enough for her to move. But she hasn't. Nor has she spoken other than to mouth *yes* or *no* in response to questions.

"Look, Beka, Shelli, a harvest moon." Katie speaks loud enough to wake up the patient in the next room. "A big, fat, red-orange moon—the biggest moon of the year." Katie unlocks the bed wheels so we can push the bed closer to the window. "Can you see it?"

Is it really the moon or is it the Phoenix rising from the ashes? I wonder. Is it a sign that both Beka and I will rise to be more magnificent than before? I tremble in delight but don't speak of the false hope it may spread around us.

The edges of Beka's lips curl.

"Remember when we were growing up and that old Mr. Meacham, who lived behind us used to sing from his work shed? It was a song about a harvest moon. Remember?" I asked.

"I remember." Katie giggles. "When he'd sing, we'd laugh as loud as we could until he'd peek his gray head over the tall hedge to sing even louder. It was always the same song. "

I think a moment. "What was that song? All I can remember is that it was about a harvest moon. Can you think of it?"

Beka rolls her eyes. "Something about…me…and my…gals." Her voice is raspy. She stares at the rising moon in its ethereal radiance.

"You're right. I remember now." I hold back my tears, look at Katie. We exchange a glance of gladness and hopefulness. Beka spoke.

I watch the bright colors wane in the rising of our harvest moon. I feel comfort remembering Mr. Meacham winking at us and then disappearing back behind the hedge to make birdhouses out of gourds, meticulously painting each one differently. "I wish we could hear him sing again and make us laugh. You know, we three haven't had a really good belly laugh in three months."

"We'll laugh again," Beka almost whispers, her voice still hoarse from the ventilator tube that sat between her vocal cords for so many days.

I thrill, again, to the sound of her voice. Katie stands beside me, we press our shoulders together hard.

As soon as Katie leaves the hospital the next morning, she calls me. "Can you get to Beka as soon as possible?"

"Why? What's wrong?" I take in a breath, fearing the worst.

"She asked to see her face in a mirror while her mom and I were there before we went to work. She was horrified by the traction and even more upset that her hair had been shaved off." Katie stops. She sounds as if she's crying. "The loss of her hair has upset her more than all her injuries."

"Did someone tell her what to expect?"

"The doctor tried but he left before a nurse brought a mirror. It was horrible. I tried to comfort her." The nurse kept suctioning out her mouth with a big plastic thing. I think if

Beka could have moved she would've popped the woman in the face."

"Did she say anything?"

"She mostly cried, but then let out a string of superlatives that made her mother run from the room. I didn't know what to do. I sat with her until she stopped weeping and fell asleep. I think the nurse gave her a sedative or something because she got sleepy really fast—before the nurse left the room.

"I have to leave now or I'll be late for work. Beka's gonna need you when she wakes up."

"I can be there in fifteen minutes."

"No wonder everyone looks at me with shocked faces." Tears flow in a meandering path down the sides of Beka's bruised, bloodied scalp staining the white sheet in pools of sepia. "I didn't know my head was shaved. Why did they shave it all?"

"I'm so sorry I didn't tell you." I swallow hard. "My guess is so they'd have a sterile field."

"Why didn't they save it?" Her voice is less raspy now. "They could have donated it to make wigs for cancer patients. Damn."

"Your life was more important than your hair at the time. Getting you into the OR was an emergency as well as an ordeal." I blot the corners of her eyes with a tissue, trying to think of something comforting to say. "Besides, if I remember correctly, you once threatened to cut it short enough for gelled spikes. You can do that in a few weeks."

"Katie reminded me of that already. Too bad I'm over that phase." Beka closes her eyes. I sit next to her bed, my mind as blank as a sky without clouds.

Several days have passed since Beka spoke her first words. Her smiles seem halfhearted. There's not even the hint of a sparkle in her eyes. She's asked about my escape from New Orleans, my diagnosis, my therapy. I've told her the parts she needs to hear. As she listens, tears trickle down the side of her face. Her tears aren't sad tears for me. She's happy for me. It's her own pain she's drowning in. I'm still having trouble believing that all of our sorrow isn't due to me. With every day that Beka doesn't move, I'm more certain that she's paralyzed. Paralyzed just like Ben Lowenstein who lived in a wheelchair for twenty-one fucking years before he died from an overwhelming urinary tract infection. Ben Lowenstein who couldn't move anything except his head. Ben Lowenstein whose mother bathed him and cleaned up his shit every day until the day he died. Ben Lowenstein who earned an asinine degree in history by picking at the computer keys with a stick in his mouth.

"Beka Schultzberg." I startle her. "You will walk out of this hospital if I have to die making it happen. Ben Lowenstein is the reason I wanted to be a doctor, and he's dead. Dead. I won't let you die, Beka, I promise you that. I won't let you die. I won't let you be paralyzed."

Beka stares blankly and I feel ashamed for making such bold statements. But I would die for her, if I could. I remember Beka at my wedding walking down the aisle in a yellow gown with a bouquet of zinnias in her hands. Walking proud, with a big smile. She will walk again. She has to walk again. Spinal Cord Rejuvenation—this is my thesis, this is supposed to be my life's work. Only I've caused the opposite, not cured it.

"That didn't come out right." I frown. "You know I'll do anything to get you on your feet. Anything." I squeeze her hand even though I know she can't feel it.

"Thanks," she whispers. "Shell?"

"What is it?" I lean closer so I can hear her whispering.

"While you were in intensive care in New Orleans, I thought you would die that first night. Seeing all your family so sad, I prayed that God would take me instead of you."

"Beka? You didn't."

"You're so special, Shelli. You have a humanitarian goal. Everybody loves you. Everyone was gathered around you. I knew I could easily fade away."

"Stop." I say through sobs. "We're equal. No, you could not easily fade away."

"I just love you so much. I couldn't stand seeing you lying there on that ventilator."

"Ditto."

We're silent for a while as I contemplate Beka's words. I'd never imagined anyone wanting to die for me, at least in the literal sense. I've always known that Beka and Katie loved me but this is overwhelming. It's time for me to start over. It's time for me to understand my life, the then and the now of it. Everything is not about me.

"Shelli?" Beka breaks the silence. I look to her in a new light. "Soon…it will be Rosh Hashanah and Yom Kippur…the New Year…the time for new beginnings." A thin tear escapes mingling with the old blood around one of the screws on the side of her head.

These don't sound like words that would pass through Beka's lips. I pause, feeling the beating of my heart in my throat. "And?"

"Maybe it would help if we read the scriptures leading up to the High Holy Days."

People who are at the end of their rope turn to religion for their salvation. Is that where Beka thinks she is? We are? My expression is one of reservation.

Beka smiles. "We need a plan. We're different now."

I'm speechless. I can't read her. Is she sarcastic? Angry? She's been so strong, she's got to be afraid of the looming possibility that she'll never walk. Then I go spouting off that I'll save her. Beginning anew. What a laugh. We've already begun anew—me in psychotherapy and her paralyzed.

"It's the least we can do." Beka pleads.

"Fine. We'll read the scriptures but I don't know where to start."

"I do." Beka's face is blank.

"How do you know?"

"Well." Beka hesitates, her eyes peering into mine. "If we really want to start over…maybe we should read the daily prayer book for Rosh Hashanah."

"*The Machzor.*" I chuckle and shake my head. "Are you certain? That's pretty heavy, isn't it?"

"I don't know. I've never read it but someone told me it would be a good place to start."

"Who might that be?" I ask, baffled.

"I can't remember, one of the doctors or counselors, I think."

"Beka…"

"Let's at least try."

"It certainly won't hurt to try. I'll get one for us."

"Mazel tov." Beka's tears make their way to her ears and I wipe them away with a tissue.

I kiss her damp cheek. "Mazel tov to you too. We will have good luck, we will."

She closes her eyes. The echo of her voice so familiar, so frail, reaches down as far inside of me as I have space to feel. My mind races, watching my friend lying still with eyes closed. What must she be thinking? What can I do except be here, by her side, crying, praying, worrying. The idea of reading the *Machzor* perplexes me. My prayers for her are wordless, feelings only, mixed up feelings of hope to a god I don't know exists. Why can't I trust that Naomi's comforting drape was sent from the god of my ancestors, the God of Israel? Misery weighs heavy. I don't know if I can carry it any longer. My shame, my guilt...my fault.

Beka clears her throat, turns to me with pleading eyes. I go to her, trying to hide my skepticism. I wipe away her tears with shaking hands already wet from my own. My whole body is trembling now. I make myself say what I hope is true. "We have to believe that there is an end to this darkness. We have to at least pretend that our dark night will slip away and we'll see the glorious light of day—that we will become two sane, whole women again. We have to be positive." I force a smile. Beka seems to do the same. Our tears blur. I press my cheek to hers and we weep. I feel a familiar hand on my back.

Katie leans down and whispers. "I don't know what you two are crying about but you can't cry without me."

Beka clears her throat again. "Our darlin' Kate."

At the sound of Beka's voice, Katie begins blubbering as well.

"Looks like I found the right place." Zack enters the room. "The three slobber sisters together again, doing what they do best."

## 19

The next morning when I enter Beka's room, I find Katie playing with her iPod. "Good morning. What's up?"

"Last night Beka said it was too quiet so I'm loaning her phone with a couple of movie soundtracks."

"Which ones?"

"*The Jazz Singer* and *Jonathan Livingston Seagull.*" Katie points her nose proudly in the air.

"Cool."

Beka smiles. "I didn't think they'd be so easy to find." Her voice is crisp and the sound of it makes me smile.

Before I can comment, Katie teases. "She asked because she can't wait to hear her dream man, Yussel, what's his name?"

"Yussel Rabinowitz," Beka says loudly this time. "He *is* the jazz singer."

"Oy vay" I say, "Your voice is back. I was beginning to like that raspy tone."

Beka rolls her eyes the way she's done since the first time she learned to roll them when she was three.

"What's with the seagull one?" I ask.

"That's one my mom used to play over and over when I was little," Beka says. "Don't you remember hearing it at my house?"

"Sounds familiar but I can't remember it. Do you, Katie?"

"I listened to it last night. I remembered one song, *Dear Father*. When you hear it you'll remember us dancing around the living room wishing we could take off flying."

"Yes, I remember now—the three of us twirling, leaping through the air." I stop, feeling sad that I'm reminding Beka of something she can no longer do.

Katie connects Beks's phone to a set of speakers before looking at her watch. "I gotta go. I'll see you after work." She kisses Beka's forehead.

"Katie," Beka says. "Thanks."

"Anything for you." Katie looks from Beka to me. "Anything for both of you."

I smile, unable to speak, as I watch Katie hurry away. "You know something?" I look at Beka. "God gave us a precious gift when we were five years old. He gave us Katie."

Beka squeezes her eyes, probably to squelch a tear.

Together we listen to the music, each drifting off into our own worlds. Two nurses come in to bathe Beka and change her bed, so I excuse myself to get a latte from the coffee shop in the lobby of the Physical Sciences' Building. While waiting in the long line, a vision appears, or maybe it's just my over-taxed imagination. I see the ocean at twilight. There's a tent made with layers of gauze fabric that's strung with hundreds of tiny white lights. Luminaries and tall torches surround it. Katie, Beka, and I are dressed in flowing white togas, our heads adorned with wreaths of flowers. We hold hands, sing joyously. We celebrate our healing with a mikvah. We celebrate our healing. We celebrate. Beka stands between us as we walk into the ocean. Walk.

While I sit beside Beka's bed, I try to keep the mikvah vision at the center of my mind. She asks me about New Orleans again, specifically my relationships there but I sense she really wants to know about the last night. I try to fill in the blanks without the gory details. I also tell her about my setbacks, including the one when she coded in the OR. No one had told her about that. One more thing to cry about. Like everybody else she says she understands. By telling my story, I worry that I'm asking too much of her to think about me and my problems while she lies here, her body still as death.

Beka interrupts my thoughts. "You said that God gave us a special gift when he gave us Katie. Do you really believe she's a gift from God?"

I blow air through my lips. "I honestly don't know why I said that. She seems like a gift."

"Well, if you think God gave her to us, you must believe that God exists." Beka's face strains as she attempts to look up to catch a glimpse of the stubble growing on her head. "If you believe that, you must pray."

"I did a lot of praying just before my wedding then again after Naomi died. You know, reading or reciting prayers I learned while I was growing up. I felt happy planning my wedding. The prayers were an overflow of my joy. When Naomi died, I needed to believe she was alive in the place we call Gan Eden. So, my prayers were really begging that the god of my ancestors was real, that He would look out for Naomi."

"What about now?"

"Now. Humm." I gather my hair into one hand, hold it away from my neck. "After all that's happened, I'm not so sure about God. My faith has never been tested until now."

"People pray when they're infirmed."

"Sickness makes people need God or something else to save them. I guess I feel alone or abandoned because of our problems." I stop to think without taking my eyes off Beka's. "Sometimes I think that feelings—happy, reflective, sad—are really prayers. At least I want to believe in a god who knows what I'm going through, a supreme being to show me how to get out of the messes I make. Does that make sense?"

Beka wrinkles her nose. "I don't think or feel that there's a god out there listening."

"Yeah. I know. Sometimes I believe in a *force* of some kind but not the god from the *Torah*."

"Lately, maybe because of our predicaments, I've tried to believe, tried to find someone to save us," Beka says. "I never really gave God a chance before, now I'm begging Him to be real and to be here for us."

"I feel the same. I, at least, lived my life on the surface, took you, Katie, Zack, my family for granted. In fact, I let the world revolve around fulfilling my dreams and desires. I was never in need, so I didn't need God."

"We're in need now, aren't we?"

"Yes but we have each other."

"Look at me, Shelli, I'm a quadriplegic. You could set the foot of my bed on fire and I would burn to death before I felt pain. Who's going to take care of me? I'm totally dependent. I'm nothing more than a head sitting on a shelf."

"Beka, don't…" My breathing is heavy, my chest feels as if it's in a vise. *It's not my fault, it's not my fault,* I repeat in my mind. "I'm sorry I invited you to come to see me. I didn't mean for this to happen to you. I'm so sorry, Beka." I try to hold back the floodgates.

"Stop, Shelli." Beka yells with about all the strength in her. "I'm not blaming you. This, oy." Beka gasps, looking at me with wide eyes that turn to pools of brown. "Shelli, listen to me. I didn't realize how you felt. Oh the pain I'm putting you through. I'm so sorry. Do you hear me? You think this is your fault, don't you?" Beka is red-faced "Well, erase that thought from your mind. You had nothing, nothing to do with my accident." As Beka tries to catch her breath, the monitor beside her bed sounds an alarm.

A tall, dark nurse who looks more like a bathing suit model rushes into the room. "What's wrong, Beka? Your heart rate just about doubled."

Beka doesn't answer as tears clog her throat. The nurse suctions Beka's nose and mouth, wipes her tears then hands me a tissue.

"Yes, I blame myself for your accident. I love you. I don't want you to be a quadriplegic. I want our lives to go back to the way we were but I don't know how to get us there."

The nurse puts her arm around me while she rubs the back of two fingers against Beka's cheek. "This must be Shelli," she says.

Beka smiles. "Yes. Isn't she everything I told you she was?"

"That and more." The nurse smiles at me. She looks like someone who would make time in her busy schedule to sit and listen. "Shelli, you didn't put Beka in this bed. Car accidents happen all the time. That's just what they are—accidents. Dr. Fitzpatrick, our attending physician, still believes Beka has a fighting chance to survive this injury completely. A fighting chance means she has to be positive and strong. Now is the time for you to be positive too. And strong." She turns to Beka. "You, young lady, forgot what we talked about this morning." The kind-faced nurse glances at me before turning back to Beka. "There may be a time for grieving but it's not now. If that time ever arrives, I'll be right here with you. I don't foresee that happening. Okay?"

"Let's just say I'm here to do my best Howie Mandel impersonation." Beka flutters her eyelashes. Her lips form a quirky grin.

"I'll see you young ladies later." The nurse says as she walks out of the cubicle shaking her head.

"You're wonderful, Beka. You're strong, so positive. I know you're afraid. I am too. All this time I've been sitting here trying to help you, and here you are helping me."

"You're making me cry again. Will you help me blow my nose? I don't want a nurse in here with that damn suction catheter."

"Tell me what to do."

"Just put a tissue over my nose. I'll try to blow into it. You can wear gloves if you don't want snot all over you."

"We're slobber sisters. Since when did your snot ever turn me off?"

She smiles then blows out through her nose while I choke back my emotions.

"Did you get it all out?"

"Yeah, I think so." Beka wrinkles her nose then sniffs again. "We'll get better, won't we?"

I clench my nails into the scars on my palms. I hold my breath until I can speak without tears. "Yeah, we will." Beka closes her eyes while I settle into a reclining sleep chair beside the bed. As I relive our conversation, I realize that the sadness I feel is normal—not detrimental. We will get better. We will.

I jerk when the room fills with student nurses and their instructor. "We're sorry to interrupt," the instructor says. "I just want to show the students Ms. Schultzberg's cervical traction." The instructor goes on about this treatment for an *unstable* fracture of the cervical spine. "This appliance is known as the Gardner Wells tongs."

Beka is staring straight up, ignoring the menagerie. How I hate teaching hospitals. When the instructor is finished with her spiel, the students thank us graciously. I can see that most of them are either embarrassed or upset by what they've seen. I clench my jaw.

Beka glances out the corner of her eye to make sure they are gone. "Damn."

"Sorry, Beka. It's a teaching hospital."

"Guess I'm the oddity of the day."

"Well, I don't know if the students learned anything today or not but I did. When I get back to med school I'm going to figure out a way to be kind to the patients when they're on display."

Beka grins. "It's okay. The instructor asked my permission yesterday. I just didn't expect to be gawked at by such a large crowd."

"Well, you should have." I chuckle. "You look like a character right out of *Dawn of The Dead*."

Beka sneers then says, "Hi, I'm Chucky, wanna play?"

I burst out in a belly laugh.

"Another thing." Beka looks at me with desperation.

"What?" I'm afraid to hear what she's going to say, afraid I've gone too far with the joking, yet I'm anxious for Beka to get some frustrations out.

"I want to talk about my career. It was just the beginning. I was on the brink of breaking through into the big time but now…"

"Once you're out of here, you can pick up where you left off. Can't you?"

"It would have to be a really big miracle. Every day I lie here, I lose touch. When I lose touch, I lose ground. Fashion design is very competitive. I can feel other rookies, like me, climbing over me. Some are glad I'm out of their way."

"But your portfolio is—"

"At a standstill. Gathering dust. By the time I get out of here, I won't know where the cutting edge is. Like Heidi Klum says, 'One day you're in. The next day you're out.' Geeze." Beka blows air into her cheeks then puffs it out. "What you don't understand is fashionability. It's a fine line—designs have to be over the top—not way over like…" Beka squints as if to find the right words or maybe just catch her breath. She hasn't spoken so much, so fast since before the accident. "Designs have to be eclectic—wearable world-wide but still be suitable for middle-class America, yet not to the point of hideous or ridiculous. If I'm not in the middle of it all, I won't know where that fine line is."

I know Beka is right. My heart is breaking for her. "With all your talent, something will work out." I don't know where these words come from or what they mean in the long-range scheme of Beka's life. She's silent, staring at the ceiling. "When I called you, before the accident, you said something about a man 'and more' in your life. What's going on that I don't know about?"

"Something. Nothing."

"What's that supposed to mean?" I stand again so I can see her eyes but she continues to stare at the ceiling

"The something was about my career, but that part is over now."

"What about the man?"

Beka sighs long and loud. She finally looks me in the eye. "I don't have everything straight in my head yet. I was thinking...about many things. Maybe I just wanted to change my strategy. But now, well, maybe I was hiding away in the world of high fashion."

"Hiding?"

"The industry is glamorous but surreal. Designing is challenging. There is...was...the excitement of being a part of it all in New York City—staying out all night, getting lots of male attention." She huffs. "It was a sham."

"Like how?"

"There was a guy. A guy who might have changed all that. We talked one afternoon. I haven't seen him since. So, he's the nothing part."

"Are you sure?"

Beka smiles for the first time today. "You and Katie are the ones who believe in predestination. So, who knows? Anyway, he just said some things that got me thinking. Talking with him was like talking to an old friend who knows everything about me, past, present, future."

"Sounds like a soul mate. Do you want to get in touch with him? Can I call him for you?"

"Remember my theory about me not being out there looking for a man but sort of waiting for one to fall into my lap?"

"Yeah."

"Well, this guy did but he scared me. He's just too wise about life." Beka stares at the ceiling again. "Anyway, look at me now. Why would he want me like this?"

I kiss Beka's forehead and excuse myself before I relapse in front of her. In the waiting room, I grab my head with both hands pulling it down until my chin crunches against my chest. Was Beka on the verge of making a commitment with a man, a man who doesn't know where she is or what's happened to her? The tailwinds of my storm are still raging out of control. *Breathe. Breathe.* I try not to feel responsible.

"Shelli?" Katie stands behind me and begins to massage my shoulders.

All I can do is sigh. "Is it five-thirty already?"

"Almost six. Shift change for us."

Katie keeps massaging while I fill her in on the happenings of the day, including Beka's revelation and my vision of the healing mikvah. "We're getting far too religious for our own good." I place my hands on hers. "Thanks for the massage. I'm better now."

When we enter Beka's room, a nurse is just finishing up her routine examination.

"So, I hear you were talking about God today," Katie beams. "The last time we talked about God was when we were five."

Beka brightens. "I remember. The first time you crossed yourself in front of us we asked what you were doing."

I laugh, remembering. "Before long we had an altar set up in my bedroom and Mama caught us genuflecting and kneeling before The Virgin to say our Hail Mary's."

"It's been a long day, Katie." Beka turns serious. Shelli and I came up with a plan.

Katie stands next to Beka's bed. "Let's hear it."

"I think, that, well, this is going to sound crazy. I really think we need to find out more about God."

"You mean the god who heals people?" Katie asks.

"That's the one. I lie here, day and night, begging to feel something but to whom am I begging?"

"I think everyone calls out to God when they're in need," Katie says softly.

"Well, Shelli and I are in need. We've decided to read the daily prayer book for Rosh Hashanah and Yom Kippur."

"The *Machzor*." I shrug. "It just might help us. When I read wedding rituals before my wedding, I felt like I was learning something about my ancestors. It was so personal that I didn't talk much about it." I stop to think. "I wasn't really relating to God or a god, it was the rituals, the history of our faith. It was a game, a very meaningful game."

Katie looks at us as if she's afraid to speak her mind. She licks her lips, wrings her hands. "When people are at the end of their rope, they often turn to religion."

"We know," Beka says. "That's about where we are."

## 20

As Beka and I begin to search for a god who can save us from our horrors, I feel even more responsible for our predicaments. When I sit before Dr. Sloan, I ramble on and he listens. "Sure, maybe there is a god out there...even if I was touched and healed and forgiven, I wouldn't feel that I deserve it." Guilt seeps from my heart to clog my pores. My skin itches. I want to scratch it raw. Why can't I get over this guilt and sadness by myself? Why do I suddenly need divine intervention? Why does Beka? We're strong. Why can't we survive on our own? Needing a god to pull us up out of the mire is completely foreign to me. It's a fanatical, protestant-holy-roller's way of dealing with something by not dealing with it at all. Just let God come clean up the mess. I don't get that, neither do I want to dodge my responsibility. I'm guilty as charged. I want to pay the bailiff for my transgressions. Anger knots my stomach. I feel a stich in my side. I want to pay for the past, pay for the mistakes I made. Am I even on the road to recovery? Sometimes I think I'd rather die. I'm exhausted trying to deal with everything. One drink, one bottle of gin and I could be free of this guilt"

Dr. Sloan interrupts my ramblings. "Gin would be the easy way out."

"In my head, everything is clear. I'm not guilty or responsible. A personality changing psychosis invaded me. Beka's accident just happened. I didn't ram my car into hers. But in my heart, every day that I sit at her bedside, and she doesn't move literally heaps guilt upon me. I am responsible. I can't live with the guilt. I can't." There are no tears to shed. I sit straight, stoic. "Another thing, what must Zack really feel about me? Why does he want to touch me? I'm filth. I'm a whore. I don't deserve him."

Dr. Sloan's hands are folded in his lap. He hasn't moved in the last five minutes or taken his eyes off mine. "Shelli, a very sharp knife has sliced you right down the middle. You've been stitched up. Pressure dressings are keeping your arteries from spurting blood. Pain medicine is running through an IV. You're going to live but it will be weeks before all the dressings can be removed and all the thousands of stitches absorbed. Exercising is painful. Coughing or even breathing is excruciating. You did not cut yourself with the knife. You did not have any control over what the knife did to you. You are healing now. Nerve endings once numb throb with life. Do you understand my analogy?"

"In my head, yes."

"Your heart is healing, just not as quickly as you want it to. The bleeding hasn't stopped yet but it's beginning to. I can see it."

My stoic exterior melts and I wonder why I even try to wear mascara. Dr. Sloan has left me with an intern. I've gone through half a box of tissues in the few minutes he's been gone. My thoughts are so jumbled that I'm not sure what I'm feeling sad about. Maybe disappointment this time, disappointment that the thought of suicide surfaced. Where's my strength? Why can't I trust? Why do I relapse so often? Why did I hurt the ones I love the most?

Dr. Sloan taps lightly before entering the room. He's nothing more than a blur. I wipe my eyes then toss the tissue toward the overflowing wastebasket. It skims the top and lands on the floor.

"Leave it. A good hard cry is beneficial. My secretary is calling someone to come get you home and stay with you."

"Because you don't trust me?" Images of my past swirl through me. He doesn't trust me. He knows I'll buy a case of TEN on my way home. He knows that I'll drink it where no one can find me to resuscitate me. He knows.

"You're as fragile as I've ever seen you. But your progress remains remarkable. Right now, I think you need a friend who loves you, not rhetoric from me. Zack, your parents, as well as your friends are all pieces to this puzzle of yours. Realizing how much they truly care for you is, I think, a key to your recovery."

For half an hour I sit with the intern who seems to be studying a journal while I wait for Zack. I try clearing my mind. I think about the ocean and the futuristic vision of the celebratory mikvah at twilight. Sometimes creative visualization helps me more than anything. The gauze tent glows warm from the hundreds of fairy lights. Inside, Beka stands. Stands without help. I stand next to her, our smiling cheeks press together. Katie is there with her camera to capture us in our blissful states— A knock interrupts my thoughts. Before I can answer, the door swings open.

"Katie." Her serene, gentle aura surrounds me immediately. An excitement stirs deep inside even before she stoops to hug me.

"I know you were expecting Zack but the secretary couldn't get in touch with him so she called your mom. Your mom's car is in the shop, and today of all days, your father has a meeting in Charlotte, so I was next on the list. I hope I'll do."

"More than ever." I cling to her, realizing how right Dr. Sloan's perception was.

"Let's get out of here. How about lunch at Tallullas? I'm taking the rest of the afternoon off."

"Good. We haven't done *lunch* since before your wedding." I recall the joyful days before all this turmoil began.

"Do you feel up to driving, or do you want to ride with me?"

"Actually, I'm exhausted. I'd rather go with you. Zack and I can come back for my car tonight."

"Difficult day today, huh?"

"Yeah. Maybe I can take a little nap in the car on the way. Then, I have some things I want to talk about."

"Great. My car is just over there."

For a brief second I see the light. Katie trusts me. After all I've done, she trusts me. The simple question, 'Do you feel up to driving, or do you want to ride with me?' is worth more than all the hours I've spent in therapy. Katie has put her trust in me. She's given me reason to trust myself.

Katie and I sit in the shade of an umbrella drinking Carolina sweet tea while I pour my heart out to her. She listens to me, bundles up all my fears, frustrations, guilt, and disappointments and throws them to the wind. I don't know how she does it but she has a way of listening—accepting everything I have to say without ever giving a word of advice. She's amazing. Before we finish our salads and kabobs I feel almost like the old me. The taste for gin is gone, my guilt relieved or at least suppressed for the moment, and I can see just how far I've come with my therapy. My session today wasn't so much a setback as some kind of breakthrough. Sitting here with Katie makes me feel alive. Seeing her smiling accepting face makes me well again. Well. I feel as if I'm being ministered to by an angel.

"I bought this for us last night." Katie pulls a book from her purse. "I stayed up half the night reading it."

"Wow. Where did you find it?"

"At Barns & Noble. It was on a table next to the checkout. I knew you guys were talking about Rosh Hashanah. I didn't want to be left out. Besides, when I started reading it, I realized how much I already know about the stories from the Old Testament."

As I leaf through the book I find essays about the High Holy Days written by Jewish women. Some of the essays question the existence of God and the validity of the Jewish tradition.

"This is great. The three of us can use this as a guide to, well, to figure out life." I look at my watch. "It's almost three. Can we take this to the hospital and get started?"

"Of course. Why did you think I suggested a restaurant in Chapel Hill?"

"Thank you for this. Let's hope the New Year brings us something to celebrate." I close my eyes to revisit my mikvah vision. I see our tent, flaps blowing in the breeze, under a violet sky. We stand together, Beka, Katie, and I, holding hands as we walk toward the ocean.

"What are you thinking about?" Katie asks, leaning toward me.

"My mikvah vision." I tell her about it, wondering if my eyes are sparkling in this afternoon sun as much as hers.

"It was a premonition, not a vision or an imagining." Katie smiles, one of her wistful smiles. "It's lovely, Shell. I can see it too. Have you told Beka about it?"

"No. I was afraid to give her too much hope."

"There's no such thing as too much hope."

When we enter the step-down unit, the receptionist announces, with a huge smile, that Beka has been moved to a regular room on the neuro unit. We rush to her new room knowing that this is an important step in Beka's progress. This unit is a new concept—Planetree. The focus is caring for mind, body, and spirit. I guess it all starts with a room that looks more like an expensive hotel than a hospital.

We're met with the aroma of flowers. Beka is propped to her side, facing us. The traction and tongs have been removed. The caked blood has been washed away to reveal a layer of auburn fuzz.

"Well, just look at you." I run my hand gently over her head. "Your hair's growing back and your head piercing is gone. Darn. I was just getting used to the new look."

"When they took the tongs out, I got a shampoo. Guess my stubble isn't stuck to my head anymore."

"Look at all the flowers." Katie twirls to take them all in. "Where did they come from?"

"I think the news got out that I died," Beka says. "Actually, the nurse said flowers weren't allowed in the step-down unit. So, when people sent flowers, the florist held them until I was moved here."

"There must be twenty bouquets."

"I guess the florist decided you were more alive than dead." I giggle.

"Shelli." Katie throws me a frown.

"It's okay, Katie." Beka laughs. "We need a little humor around here. Even though I appreciate these flowers, could you take all but the one with the big yellow bow away? I kind of feel like I'm in funeral home."

"This one with the yellow bow is a plant, calla lilies. Nice." Katie looks to see who sent it. "There's no card. Who's it from?"

"Humm...can't remember. I asked one of the nurse's aides to take the cards off after reading them to me. I'm not really sure who that one is from, I just liked—"

"Your favorite flowers and the yellow bow." Katie smiles.

"Yeah." Beka smiles back. "I do love yellow."

"Look what Katie got for us." I hold the book up in front of Beka.

"I found it by accident," Katie says. "I didn't want to be left out of your discussions. That is, if it's okay with you guys."

"Fine with me. You probably know more about religion than Shelli and I put together. Now that I can face you, why don't you pull some chairs up so we can see eye-to-eye."

"You look so much better today. I like the new bed too." I try not to be overly excited. I feel as if I will break into tears. I wonder if this is the way Beka will live the rest of her life.

"It's still a hospital bed but it can be lowered practically to the ground."

"Cool," I say.

Katie pulls a chair close to the head of the bed. "So what have you talked about so far? What have I missed?"

"We didn't get very far." Beka looks to me. "We talked about how important rituals are in people's lives."

"The real truth is that we're trying to see if there's a god out there who can heal us. Right, Beka? We're getting desperate." I suck in my bottom lip. "There are lots of rituals for Rosh Hashanah, so we started reading the prayer book for the days leading up to the High Holy Days. The first reading is Genesis 21." I take in a big breath, feeling a little self-conscious. "It's about Abraham and Sarah having a son in their old age. We're trying to understand what this story has to say to us."

"I know the story. I remember the nuns telling it. Sarah was ninety and barren. She laughed at God when he told her she would bear Abraham's son."

"But the story starts before that," I tell her. "God made a covenant with Abraham that if Abraham followed Him, He would make him patriarch of a great nation."

"Sure." Beka lets out a humph. "So Abraham wanders in the desert dragging poor Sarah behind him for how many decades? I can't remember."

Katie looks at Beka with her eyes squinted. "God promised Abraham a son."

"We're getting ahead of ourselves here." Beka stops to think. "First God leads Abraham from one place to the next for who knows what reason. They settle, he and Sarah, somewhere in the desert but there's a famine, so God leads them to Egypt. Sarah was evidently gorgeous and ol' Abe thinks the Egyptian Pharaoh will want to get his hands on her and kill him. So, does he trust God to direct him? No way. He says Sarah is his sister. He offers her to the dirty—"

"Really?" Katie's eyes are as big as our harvest moon.

"Really." Beka blinks her dark lashes a few times before taking a breath. "So while the Pharaoh is making it with Sarah, Abe has been rewarded with herds and servants. Just guess who the main servant is—the Pharaoh's own daughter Hagar."

"Wait." Katie looks exasperated as she dishevels her hair by running both hands through it. "I thought Abraham loved Sarah."

"More like Sarah loved Abraham. He took advantage of her." Beka grimaces. "In her old age, she worries that God isn't keeping up with His part of the bargain because she hasn't conceived. So she tells Abraham to go make a baby with Hagar, his concubine."

"Hagar wasn't a concubine, was she?" I ask. "I thought she was Sarah's handmaiden."

"She was Sarah's handmaiden and Abe's ho. Shelli, honestly. Don't be so naive." Beka frowns. "Sarah was used by almost everyone."

"Everyone?" Poor Katie is flushed now.

"Yes. Used by God, Abe, the Pharaoh, and Hagar."

"Now, I'm as confused as Katie. I thought…I don't know what I thought."

"This is how the story goes." Beka scrunches her eyelids. I realize how much I miss her animation. For a moment, I'm far away. Worried sick. I choke back vomit and tears.

"Can you imagine how Sarah felt when Hagar gave Abe the son of his heart?"

"But God promised Sarah a son and she had Isaac soon after," Katie speaks to Beka then turns to me for some sort of reassurance.

I raise my eyebrows, speechless.

"Right but here's the kicker—Ishmael. Hagar's son was first born and Abe loved him best. Sarah could see it. She was afraid Ishmael would steal Isaac's birthright, so she had Hagar and Ishmael banished to the desert."

Katie looks more puzzled than ever. "Why would God allow that?"

"Allow what?" Beka asks.

"Allow Abraham to have sons with Hagar and Sarah?"

Beka blows air into her cheeks until she looks like a blowfish.

"Listen to this," I say, trying to get us back on the subject. "This first essay starts out with, 'And the Lord remembered Sarah.' What does that mean?"

"Do you think Sarah made a mistake by deciding that God had *forgotten* her and offered Hagar to bear sons for Abraham?" Katie says. "Or, after Hagar gave birth to Abraham's son, did God suddenly *remember* His promise to Sarah?"

"Now, do you see where I'm coming from?" Beka asks. "If God promises something, how can He forget? Isn't He omniscient? Why would He want Sarah to suffer?"

Katie speaks slowly as if she's seeing this scripture in a new light. "Sarah must have felt humiliated to be pregnant at ninety."

"So, it must have been an act of the ole' holy God," Beka states, "to let an old woman get pregnant. Abraham was one hundred. If Ishmael and Isaac were Abraham's sons, there must have been some Cialas around.

"Beka." Katie snaps. "It's a miracle. The whole Judeao-Christian and Islamic traditions descend from Abraham."

"At whose expense?" Beka is red-faced as she glares at Katie. "Sarah's and Hagar's, that's whose. Women have been used by God in these *miraculous* biblical stories since the beginning of time. How can anyone have faith in God when the scriptures are full of this nonsense?"

"We could argue that one until death. Still, if this story is true, it *is* a miracle." Katie says.

"Well then Sarah didn't have faith in God either," I say, "or else she wouldn't have made that decision."

"They had to do it to fulfill the covenant of the fathers of the Jews and Arabs," Beka says. "That being Abraham on both accounts. Sounds fishy to me. The point of the story, or of history, is that Abraham is the father or patriarch of both the Arabs and the Jews and that all the strife between the two nations is nothing more than sibling rivalry."

Katie and I laugh. "Beka. We're trying to be serious."

"So am I," Beka states rather matter-of-factly. "Sarah, fearing that her son won't inherit his birthright, convinces Abraham to banish Hagar and her son Ishmael to the desert where they nearly die. The mothers were already engaged in a rivalry."

"So, Sarah is ugly to Hagar, and we Jews embrace her as the mother of us all," Beka states. "That's why I've never been able to buy into Judaism. That and a whole lot of other biblical bull stories."

"Beka." Katie raises her voice.

"Sorry, Katie, but that's why I've never *embraced* my faith."

Katie looks distressed.

"Katie…" I stop to think, try to unlearn the message this scripture held for me, try to put myself first into Sarah's place, then into Hagar's. "This scripture was always about Abraham and his willingness to sacrifice Isaac." I reflect on memories from my days in Hebrew school. "I've never really thought about what Sarah and Hagar went through."

"Sarah and Hagar didn't make up, did they?" Beka raises her eyebrows. "So what can Sarah teach us?"

"Forgiveness." Katie looks at her lap as silence surrounds us. She finally continues. "Maybe Sarah and Hagar didn't make up, maybe they wanted to but had too much pride or maybe even pain. This is going to sound preachy but just think about it a minute." Katie's face pales as she draws in a deep breath. "We all struggle with conflicting emotions. We've all, at some point in our lives, felt like throwing a piece of ourselves into the wilderness to die. That's what Sarah did to Hagar." Katie looks sternly into my eyes then Beka's. "Part of what you call teshuvah is about identifying with Sarah and forgiving her."

"I think I get it," I say. "Teshuvah is repentance, an important ritual between Rosh Hashanah and Yom Kippur. I want to throw all the ugly things I did into the wilderness to disintegrate. Man, I can identify with her there."

"Not just you, Shell, all of us need to identify with her." Katie moves to stoop next to my chair. "Isn't that what Rosh Hashanah means? We've all sinned. There was a time I wanted to banish you to the wilderness. I'm sorry I didn't have empathy then."

Katie's words stab at my heart and I know I deserve to hear them.

"Isn't the first step..." Katie stops, closes her eyes. "Isn't the first step taking the blame for our misfortunes away from God?"

I look at Beka. "I'm angry as well, for all of this, for everything. Maybe that's why we can't believe in God."

"We all have doubts right now. We want to blame God for everything but we're not even sure that God exists," Katie says. "Still I go to mass so I can light candles for both of you. I don't want either of you to suffer anymore. I wish I could trade places with both of you."

"Oh, Katie." I wrap my arms around her. "You don't deserve all the pain we're laying on you." Katie holds tightly and for the first time, at least in front of us, she breaks down.

Beka's monitor alarms blare. Katie and I turn to see Beka's red, tear-stained face.

"She's choking," Katie yells.

I grab the suction catheter to suction out the back of Beka's throat before the nurse comes flying in. "We have to make a pledge not to cry in here anymore," I suggest.

Beka swallows, takes in a deep breath.

"Great job," a nurse I hadn't seen before says. "Where did you learn to do that?"

"Do what? Suction her or cause her to choke to death?" I look at Katie, roll my eyes.

"She learned it in medical school." Katie says. "She's going to be a doctor."

The nurse pats Beka's shoulder, looks at her IV, feels her hands and feet before walking out of the room without so much as a smile or word of concern.

"Who was that?" I ask.

"Nurse Ratched," Beka says. And we laugh.

When Zack meets me in front of the main hospital entrance, we decide to wait until tomorrow morning to retrieve my car from Dr. Sloan's parking lot. I tell Zack a little about today but I'm so exhausted that I sit in silence pondering all that's happened—my relapse, Katie's trust, Beka's new room, our search for the meaning of our tribulations, and the meaning of life in general. "Nurse Ratched," I say.

Zack flashes a frown.

"It was the best part of the day."

"What was?"

"Today was an emotional rollercoaster. We all hit bottom but in the end we laughed about something frivolous. For just a moment we were carefree." I smile, remembering. "Carefree…"

## 21

Katie and I sit in Beka's room to continue the conversation we began yesterday. Beka is propped on her side again so it's easier for her to communicate with us.

"Yesterday I think we got a little off the subject as well as a lot off our chests." Katie pulls up a chair close to the head of Beka's bed. Maybe we need to focus on finding some kind of meaning because of all that's happened. You know what people say, everything happens for a reason."

"I'm starting to believe that...in a way. If there is a god, where is he? I never see him." Beka stares at Katie with fire in her eyes.

Katie touches Beka's shoulder. "I don't see God in church probably the same way you don't see Him in the synagogue. But, I'm carrying a miracle right here." Katie pats her belly then turns to reach out for me. "There are other moments of wonder that, to me, seem like a god or some supreme creator—hearing both of you laugh, feeling the pain of your broken hearts, the joy of sunrises and sunsets, the wind in the trees, the flowers, the ocean. Isn't that...*God's voice* telling us that He is with us through thick and thin. My faith isn't in the Catholic Church. It's in the Creator of the universe. We're all a part of that unity, always have been, always will be."

Silence embraces us as Katie's words seep into our fragile minds.

Beka breaks the silence. "I want to believe what you believe. But I don't—not yet.

"So, what is it, Beka? What are you thinking?" Katie leans forward.

"If everything happens for a reason," Beka says, "then it has to happen for a good reason. Right?"

Katie and I stop to think.

"I want to believe that there's something better for me," Beka explains. "I don't think it's this bed. It's something else. I don't even know what it is but I'm feeling relieved that I don't have to go back to New York. I don't have to live in that frantic world that blocks out the real me, whoever I am. I needed an excuse to let it go. Maybe this *accident* is my excuse, so let's pray to the god I'm trying to find that something good will come of this mayhem."

"What is it, Beka?" I move closer to her. "Something's going on with you and has been since before the accident. Why can't you tell us?"

Beka rubs her tongue along her bottom lip then smiles at us. "I guess it's time. I met someone at a party. Someone insightful." Beka wears a nervous smile. Her eyes glisten. "I wasn't holding anything back from you, honestly. I was so excited to tell you all about him as soon as I got here. I'd been keeping him a secret because he was so different from all the other men I've been interested in."

"Who is he?" I ask. "I knew you were serious over this guy."

The corners of Beka's mouth begin to curl.

"Tell us." Katie's face is radiant.

"Right now there's nothing to tell. We met one weekend this summer. I've not seen him since. He was on vacation. He's been calling me for weeks. He's very wise. That's all I've got to say."

Katie grabs my arms. "He sent the calla lilies."

Beka's face breaks into a smile.

I let out a screech. "All this time you were letting us believe you wanted to keep that one plant because it has a big yellow bow. Beka. Who is he? How does he know you're here?" I'm so happy I could burst. "He even knew your favorite flower and favorite color."

"Nice he remembered it," Katie adds, almost jumping now.

"The day after we met, I wore a yellow gown in a wedding."

Katie and I look toward each other, curiously.

"You met him at my wedding?" I ask.

"No, we met the day before your wedding, in Zack's back yard."

"Is he a friend of Zack's?"

"Well, yes. He's a hell of a wreck from Georgia Tech but he's not an engineer."

"Barry Stein?"

Beka giggles.

"No wonder you want to play *The Jazz Singer* all the time," Katie says. "You're in love with the real Yussel Rabinowitz."

"Oh my God." I laugh. "Does Zack know about this?"

"Honest guys, this is the first secret I've kept from the two of you. At first, he just called. I don't tell you about every phone call I get. After you went to New Orleans, Shelli, he showed me what a good listener he is. Lately, I've sworn Zack to secrecy. I didn't tell him about our friendship—Barry did."

"Why did you keep him such a secret?" Katie looks wounded.

"After talking with him a few times, I felt ready to at least think about changing some things in my life, in my career. The more we talked about life and the meaning of it, the more frightened I was. He had me figured out from first glance." Beka stops, asks for a sip of water. "It took our discussions about faith to let me see that my life wasn't rewarding or meaningful. I was thinking about making a change then the accident sealed it." Beka looks away. "Now, I have to make one. At least things regarding my career are clearer now."

"Maybe we could have helped you," I say hesitantly.

"You're helping me now. So, where do I go from here? I'm angry that I can't move. I'd like to think that I'm angry at

God. But then, I don't believe in God, or do I? I keep blaming Him for my condition."

While I sit with teary eyes, Katie speaks. "So, is Barry the reason you wanted to talk about religion?"

"Barry's the reason. What he says makes sense now—it didn't before the accident." A dreamy smile covers Beka's face. "The doctors said that as soon as my neck was mobilized and the swelling was gone, I'd begin to feel tingling in my fingers and toes. That should have happened days ago. But I feel nothing." Beka is fighting tears. I put my hand on her lifeless hip. "I have to learn how to live like this, to live like Ben Lowenstein." Tears flood Beka's eyes. I grab a tissue.

"Blow your nose quick before you choke and that scary nurse comes back in here." I hold a tissue to her face. Beka blows her nose and lets out a moan that makes my stomach ache. Katie looks as if she might faint. She fans her face with her hand. "What are you going to do with Barry?"

"I don't know," Beka speaks between gasps. "We still talk. He calls every night at nine-thirty. The physical therapist…gave me a headset. The nurses put it on me when his calls come in."

"Really?" I look at Katie, who seems as surprised as I do.

"He's been wonderful, even before—when I was trying to ignore him. That's what I had on my mind while on my way here. I couldn't wait to see both of you. I wanted to tell you as soon as the three of us got together so you could help me make some decisions." Beka closes her eyes. Her lips form a worried frown. "It looks like another decision has been made for me. I can't let Barry see me like this. He's a great guy. He deserves a girlfriend who's not an invalid."

Every day I worry more over Beka's lack of progress. Today she had an MRI that showed her vertebrae in alignment and her spinal cord in one piece although flattened slightly in a couple of places. The doctors wonder if the flattening of the cord is the reason she is still paralyzed. The youngest doctor, the adolescent-looking intern, says the flattening may not be permanent, that there's still hope. That's an intern for you, a doctor whose ink isn't yet dry on his diploma spouting miracles.

As our discussion continues, the problem Beka and I have is not only believing in God but also believing in a god who forgives. While we try to see a divine loving being, we are caught up in a god who wreaks havoc. Katie thinks that we can find a universal god who isn't just about forgiveness but trust, something almost impossible for Beka and me at this point. Especially if we agree with Katie that 'everything happens for a reason'.

"I've done a little research," Katie tells us, sitting up straight, her face radiant with the glow of pregnancy. "I've concluded that the relationship between God and Abraham was a constant test of trust."

"How?" Beka asks.

"Well, Abraham left his home with complete trust in God. The story seems to be true about the Pharaoh and Sarah but Abraham gave her to Pharaoh to protect both her and him."

"Explain that. I'm not following you." Beka looks perplexed.

Katie continues, "I don't think this was an uncommon practice back then, particularly since Abraham was so wealthy and his possessions could be confiscated."

"Wait a—" Beka shrieks.

"Just listen a minute." Katie scoots to the edge of her chair. "By telling the Pharaoh that Sarah was his sister, the Pharaoh accepted her into his palace where she would be safe. He then rewarded Abraham with gifts. Here's the best part—God brings hardships on the Pharaoh to get him to release Sarah and thus makes retribution to Abraham. I think

Abraham knew all along that God was watching over him and Sarah. In other words, Abraham trusted God all along. He obeyed Him by giving up Sarah."

"Gibberish." Beka wails. "We can't see God working like that now, so we have no reason to believe he did then. All these stories are religious dogma, nothing more than fairytales. I can't believe that God would promise Sarah a child and then not give her one until she was ninety. People didn't even live that long back then."

"I'm not a theologian but can you just focus on this one thing?" Katie lets out a huff. "Our whole discussion started with God remembering Sarah on the first day of Rosh Hashanah. Maybe you both have to trust that God, or a god, or whoever created the universe remembers you."

"Hmm. So, where does this bring us?" Beka seems to be pondering Katie's statement. "We've studied all the scriptures during these days leading up to Rosh Hashanah." She stops to catch her breath. "Everything is just the same. God doesn't remember us. There's no god to remember us. Shelli can't survive without a bottle of pills and a shrink and I'm just a bump on a log. You can't stop feeling sorry for us. Damn. I don't like the way things are going for us."

While Katie commiserates with Beka, I sit in the waiting room feeling angry, wondering if we should have started this quest for enlightenment that has only added to Beka's burden. So much for the Planetree theory—holistic healing, the laying on of hands. This place can't heal Beka's spine, let alone her mind, and her spirit is more broken than her neck.

The last few squares of Beka's quilt sit on my lap while my fingers furiously stitch one square to the next. My mental acuity isn't here today. My anger is rising. Maybe I should have stayed with Beka and listened to Katie. Can't Beka see that I'm moving forward with my therapy? Or does she see my progress and the lack of her own? After all we're supposed to be healing together.

"Shelli." Katie's whisper startles me. "Beka's asleep. Can I help?"

"Just one more square," I say. "I need to keep busy."

Katie watches my quick stitches. "Are you okay?"

"I thought I was until Beka's outburst."

"I know." Katie sits beside me. "She's bound to break down once in a while."

"What do you mean?"

"She's to the depression stage," Katie says tenderly. "Even in her depression she still wants you to be healthy. I think her words were honest. She's afraid that neither of you will ever be the same."

"You're right. I'm glad you were here. That statement just hit me the wrong way. It sounded like Beka can't see my progress, or that she's jealous of it." I hang my head, put the sewing down, turn to face Katie squarely. "I'm angry that she's not better."

"It's alright to be angry," Katie says. "I don't believe that God selectively intervenes in people's lives. He's not to blame for our tragedies any more than He's to blame for our triumphs."

"What you say seems plausible, yet what about predestination or everything happening for a reason? I'm so confused." I grab my hair. "Beka remembers Ben. She's afraid she'll end up the same way he did. She wants to live. She doesn't want to be paralyzed but she's afraid that's her fate. Because of Barry, she began questioning her faith, her reason for being on this earth, and lots of other personal issues. She said that she was on the verge of making some very important life changes but the accident put a stop to them."

"She was at a crossroads that's for sure. Do you think the accident was a catalyst for change?"

"Seems pretty cruel to me. It doesn't seem that we've made any progress. What are we going to do?"

"Take one day at a time, see what gets thrown at us." Katie sighs.

"Buck up like usual, huh?"

"Yeah. There's strength in numbers. One day at a time. Just like the quilt—one square at a time."

"You're awesome, you know."

"Thanks," Katie says looking down, brushing her hand over the quilt we made for Beka. "Do you think Beka will like it?"

"I know what you're thinking," I say. "Yes, she'll love it."

"You don't think it will remind her of what she once was and isn't now?"

"I hope not. I hope it will be a souvenir of a gift she gave us so selflessly."

"What do you think about Barry? Has Zack said anything?" Katie asks as she gently folds the fabric and places it in a plastic bag.

"Zack said that Barry was quite enamored with Beka at our wedding. But she was a challenge to him once she went back to New York. He tried to visit her or get her to visit him in Miami but she always had an excuse."

"Why did she keep him a secret for so long?"

"I think she's in love with him. I also think that he's in love with her." I smile at that thought. "I don't know what was going on in her head before the accident but she's afraid he won't want her if she's paralyzed."

"Maybe she won't be paralyzed."

"I hope you're right. Barry sounds like a spiritual mentor. I wonder if he wanted us to talk about religion as much for my sake as Beka's."

"Probably. I think he must know that neither of you can separate God from scriptures."

"Maybe that's God's plan for Barry." I smile. "Or maybe Barry is our salvation and God doesn't have anything to do with it."

"I remember seeing them together at your wedding but I didn't put two and two together." Katie shakes her head. "He seems to know a lot about religion—like Yussel Rabinowitz." Katie smiles. "Does Zack tell you what Barry and Beka talk about?"

"No. He's pretty good at being a confidant."

"I hope Barry is God's plan for Beka." Katie stands to leave. "Tell Beka that I love her. I'll be back tomorrow morning before work."

As Katie strolls toward the elevator my eyes fill with tears, for the pain I've put her through. Everything has been me, me, me—and Beka, Beka, Beka—while poor Katie has been holding us together. Katie has been our salvation. If I've learned anything from our sessions on Rosh Hashanah, it's been empathy. I think of Psalm 21, *And God remembered Sarah.* I close my eyes to pray, "If there is a god out there, please remember Katie and heap blessings on her."

After I sit for a few more minutes, I look at my watch. I know I must head home too. So, I meander slowly back to Beka's room, hoping that a miracle awaits me there.

Beka's eyes are closed. I clear my throat.

She turns her head toward me. "Shelli, about earlier, I didn't mean—"

"No apologies. There's nothing to apologize for."

"Still, I feel bad."

"So do I but not about what you said," I move close to the bed so Beka doesn't have to strain her eyes to see me. "We all have our up days and our days filled with…hopelessness."

"You can say that again."

"Sorry I woke you. Go back to sleep. I'll see you mid-morning tomorrow. I have an appointment with my…shrink at nine. Katie will be here before work. She said to tell you she loves you. So do I."

Beka closes her eyes. I stand by the door for several minutes watching her until I'm certain she's asleep. As I turn to go, a smile comes to my face. I realize I've been looking at Beka with my heart, not my scientific, soon-to-be-doctor mind. Why have I been comparing Beka to Ben? Beka's spine is not severed—it just received a terrible blow. There's no reason to believe that when the steroids have done their job the nerves will have enough space to conduct neurons. Yes. I go to Beka and touch her foot.

"Shelli?" she responds.

"Did you feel that?" I ask.

"Feel what?"

She felt it, even if not consciously. She felt my hand and it wore her up. I smile.

"Feel what?" she asks again.

"I blew you a kiss. It landed on your nose."

"Yeah, I felt it." She fakes a sneeze.

"Go back to sleep. I'll see you tomorrow."

As I head for the elevator, I think about all that's happened today. An amazing sense of trust engulfs me. I want to trust that the God of the universe will lead me to a safe shore. I want to trust Dr. Sloan to lead me to complete saneness. I want to trust Zack to love me, just the way I am. I want to trust in the naïve young intern who believes that Beka will walk out of here. I want to believe that I can beat this psychosis forever. My heaviness of heart floats from me as the magnificence of Naomi's sparkling drape consoles me. I don't care if this comfort is an ecstatic experience or if the God of my ancestors has visited me but I suddenly feel as if we've been remembered—Beka, Katie, Sarah, Hagar, and me. God remembers us!

I feel as if I'm hanging on for dear life as I'm swirled through the universe, picked up from my former life and dropped into this new one. In this new world, I see the edge of heaven and hear old Mr. Meacham's voice singing, *shine on, shine on, harvest moon, for me and my gals.* Is this God's voice speaking to me through one who took time to entertain three giggling girls? The words, *shine on, shine on, harvest moon, for me and my gals,* does that mean that Beka, Katie, and I will be whole—in every meaning of that word—and together throughout eternity?

I feel like shouting but I whisper instead. "The glorious light of day is coming, Beka. Soon it will be light."

As I drive home from the hospital, I feel like a firefly that's just been released from a glass jar. I realize I haven't been bothered by guilt or sadness or pain today. Is everything healing at once? Joy and a ravenous sexual hunger emerge. I imagine ways to entice Zack tonight. Even that thought comes with pleasure, not guilt. In my mind, Zack's face is crisp and I can't envision Gregoire, Jonathan, or Rosalie. Their faces are in shadows and blurs. Before they disappear completely, I embrace them. I forgive myself for the disruption I caused in their lives. My journey has taken a turn. My heart is full. Before I sleep tonight, I'll write a note to Gregoire, tell him my story, ask his forgiveness, and send my heartfelt apology for causing so much havoc in his life. Hopefully, the letter will reach him. Who knows how much devastation he has endured since I ripped his world apart.

Watermelon and yellow. The colors come swirling, replacing my darkness. I'm growing stronger by the minute. My friends and family have led me through the darkness. They stand in front of me with open arms. I *am* beginning anew. For the first time since Naomi's funeral, I see a purpose in my life. Love overflows my being.

When I open the door to our apartment, I'm treated to candlelight and a savory aroma from the kitchen. "You beat me home. What a welcome sight you are—this is," I say, looking at a vase of zinnias surrounded by candles in rose-colored votives. I take in a deep breath through my nose before I'm hit with apprehension. "Uh oh, have I missed something? I mean are we celebrating something I've forgotten?"

"Wipe that panicked look off your face. You haven't forgotten a thing. We're celebrating my first bonus. The Prague project went through."

"It did?" I say, relieved, remembering the last time Zack tried to celebrate something with me. "Congratulations." I throw down my purse and move to embrace him. We hold each other tightly, kissing the way we did on our wedding day. Him, I suppose, hungry for me, and me feeling positive to the verge of happiness. When at last our mouths separate enough to speak, I whisper, "I have just what you want for a celebration gift."

"Oh really?" he says, taking a step back but not releasing me.

Suddenly, I'm feeling embarrassed. I bite my lower lip. "Will you dance with me tonight? I mean really, really dance?" My cheeks feel warm all of a sudden.

"Are you sure?"

"Things are pretty well healed, I think. It's been almost two months since I was sewn back up." I smile up at his misty, hazel eyes with their hints of green reflecting the candlelight. "There's just one way to find out. I'm ready. Besides, I want you, Zack."

"Do you want me for hors d'oeuvres or dessert?"

I look behind him to the kitchen.

"Hors d'oeuvres, if it won't spoil dinner."

"It'll make dinner even better."

"Alrighty then," I say, unbuttoning his shirt.

"Just let me tend to a couple of things. The potato-leek soup is almost ready. Let me turn it off until later."

"So you're a mucky-muck now?"

"Not yet but don't you worry, missy, I'll be one of those mucky-mucks someday."

"You're already a mucky-muck around here."

"You think I don't know that?" Zack runs his fingers through his hair letting it hang over his eyes like a GQ model.

I move to plant my palms on his chest and a kiss on his cheek.

Zack pulls me to him. I feel his warm breath on my neck. A lightness returns. He lifts my chin, we kiss each other's lips in a way we haven't done for months, the kiss lasts and I don't ever want to break away from the familiarity of it.

I think about the hurdle I jumped today. My past has been put into perspective. So many good people have been supporting me and there's a possibility of a god who will always remember me. Later, we'll celebrate my milestone but right now Zack deserves every part of me. I'm ready to give myself freely to this man I've trampled and abused.

"Shell." Zack runs his hands up under my sweater. "Every day, every minute, you're more my girl."

"It just seems like old times, doesn't it?"

"Feels like old times too." Zack has my bra unfastened. His touch is as blind to my scars as are his eyes.

We stop in the doorway to the bedroom.

"Is it safe to go all the way?" Zack grimaces. "I don't have a condom."

Contraception hasn't been high on my priority list and even if it was, my doctor didn't think now was a time to restart my birth control pills due to my mood swings. I think a minute. "There's a can of contraceptive foam in the bathroom cabinet that's never been opened. We can use that." I stare, wistfully into Zack's anxious face. "I want to make you happy tonight. I want to please you. I'm sorry for being so wrapped up in myself and Beka. You've been so patient. I appreciate that more than you know."

Zack fumbles with the foam as we fall onto the bed, struggling to undress while our lips cling. He is gentle with me and just like our first time the physical sting turns to pleasure too soon as a surprisingly premature orgasm causes me to tremble. Zack's climax thunders through me and his body shudders as he wraps himself around me. My worry that I'll never be able to enjoy sex again is extinguished. We hold each other, lost in bliss. I am healing.

## 22

When I burst through Beka's doorway this morning, I'm hit with the aroma of chamomile and roses. Beka is dressed in Chinese silk pajamas—bright red brocade with black frog buttons. She asks if she looks freaky.

"No, but I swear your hair is growing out as red as Katie's."

"Maybe I'll never have to dye it again. Shelli?"

"What?"

"Do I really look...presentable?"

"What are you talking about? What's going on?"

Beka smiles. "Last night I finally consented to see Barry. He said he'd hop the first plane he could get. Did I do the right thing?"

"Oh my God. I can't believe it. Yes. Yes, you did the right thing."

"That's what Katie said too. Still, I feel nervous."

"What time do you expect him?"

"Soon. He flew into Raleigh about an hour ago, so he should be here...soon." A crooked smile creeps across Beka's face.

"What made you change your mind about seeing him?"

Before she can answer, we hear a tap on the door, then his voice. Our eyes glued to each other's like when we were teenagers and didn't know whether to laugh out loud or run.

"Beka." Barry greets her excitedly. He carries a huge bouquet of multi-colored calla lilies—two maybe three dozen. He leans to kiss her cheek and holds the flowers close to her nose so she can smell them. "I like the haircut," he says. "Chic."

I smile.

"Shelli, sweetheart." Barry lays the flowers on the bedside table and throws his arms around me. "You look great. A little skinny maybe but I love your rosy cheeks."

"Thank you." I step back, look to Beka. "I'll see you later. Have Barry call me if you need something."

"I will."

"You don't have to leave because of me," Barry says.

"Oh yes, I do. Beka and I are getting tired of each other's company." Beka's coy expression tells me just how serious she is about Barry. Beka and coy don't go together.

Barry holds my elbow. "I talked to Zack on my way in. Looks like I'll be your house guest for the holidays."

"Great," I say. I want to ask him how he got out of his duties for the biggest celebration of the year but guess I'll hear all about it later. I stand beside the door eavesdropping until I hear Beka laughing. I don't want to leave but I do. This moment is for Beka and I'm holding my breath for her.

Barry spent the rest of the day with Beka before heading to our townhouse. When he arrived, I was soaking in the tub and left Zack to entertain him. Whatever happened today, I want to hear it first from Beka.

This morning, Barry rode to the hospital with me. He's quite the talker and listener and quite humorous. Although he's a cantor, he admits he can't sing or chant like Neil Diamond did in *The Jazz Singer*.

Beka and I pretend to hold that against him. Beka is radiant again today, dressed in a short, soft yellow cotton nightgown.

I use the excuse to call my advisor at Duke to duck out of Beka's room for a few minutes. To my surprise, he asks me to come into the office right away to fill out the necessary forms for my reentrance into class. I'm glad to have an excuse to leave Beka and Barry alone for the whole afternoon.

After meeting with my advisor, I stroll through Duke Gardens, making my way to the gothic chapel where I sit in one of the back pews and listen to the majestic pipe organ as someone practices.

I've never been inside this chapel. I'm surprised to feel gooseflesh as the warm glow from the massive stained glass windows engulfs me. Surely a god is in this place, even for the benefit of a Jew. I'm filled with emotion as if all this beauty washing through me is mine. It's a mikvah of sorts. I try to remember a prayer or poem or scripture to express what I feel as I merge into this ambiance in much the same way I merged into the ocean in the days leading up to my wedding. Suddenly the music stops and I hear the cover of the organ close followed by the click of someone's heels on the floor as they walk away. A welcoming silence surrounds me. I see my life's plan laid out before me. I will be a doctor. I will be part of the team that finds the answer to spinal cord rejuvenation. I am inspired once again by Christopher Reeve's dream: *At first, dreams seem impossible, then improbable, and eventually inevitable.* Yes. Inevitable. I feel as if I've been reborn in this apostolic place. I have a reason to live, a reason to go back to med school, a reason to love the people who love me, a reason to love the people who refuse to let me go.

It's late afternoon on the eve of Yom Kippur. Beka and Barry are napping—his head nested next to hers as he leans from a chair beside the bed. I pace outside Beka's door remembering the laughter as she and Barry joked this afternoon. As the last rays of the sun cross my path from the hall window, warm hands caress my neck. Zack's hands.

"Hello, baby," he says. "How's my girl?" I turn to his patient, loving arms.

"I feel well, thanks to you and...everybody." I smile through happy, teary eyes. "I'm starting my fourth year of med school on Monday."

"Monday? Wow. Not next term?"

"My advisor said that if I can catch up, there's a good chance I can graduate with my class."

"Congratulations, baby. I know you can do it." Zack lifts me off the floor and swings me around the way he did when we were teenagers.

"This afternoon, we were feeling goofy...thinking about ways we could change the world. We got a little carried away. Beka said if she could master a computer with a wand in her mouth she could become an astronaut. She's so positive today."

Zack smiles as he looks toward Beka's room. "So, how are they? Did something else happen to make you so, giddy?"

"Like what? Do you know something I don't know?"

"Barry's torn. He's smitten but Beka won't let him go there."

"Just seeing them together is awesome. They talk non-stop and laugh at everything. He seems more than a mentor. He complains as much about Judaism as she does."

"Barry's more spiritual than religious, I think. But there's no doubt he believes in God. He and Beka are good friends. He knows how confused she is."

"Yeah, I could see that this afternoon."

"He's been good for her, and me." Zack takes a step back letting his hands slip from around my shoulders down to my hands. "He's helped me through so much, especially before you had a diagnosis."

"All this time I thought Barry came to save Beka," I say. "Sounds like he's been working on you too."

"We've had some interesting discussions."

"About faith?"

"Yeah. About how maybe I could use a little."

Zack lets go of one hand and twirls me around with the other. "Katie, Sean, Hello."

"Ahh, if it isn't the little love birds," Katie says. "How's it going today?"

"Just fine, little mama. How's our little Laura-Kate?"

Katie pats her belly. "Rambunctious. I think you were right about us having a baby who'll love football. She's been practicing kicking field goals all day. Look at this." Katie hands Zack a big plastic bag then pulls a paper from her purse. "First baby picture. I had an ultrasound today. She's a Laura Katherine, alright, or else a poorly endowed little boy. Look." She hands me the ultrasound picture. "Those are her legs and her little butt cheeks, right there, see?" Katie points to the pelvis. "She's a girl."

"Congratulations," I say, feeling a sudden twinge of jealousy. "I'm so happy for both of you."

"Thanks. How's Beka? I can't wait to show her this picture and, oh, I forgot, I finished the edging on the quilt last night." Katie removes the quilt from the bag and hands each of us a corner. We all step back until it's unfolded. I gasp when I see the brilliance. It reminds me that our lives, Katie's, Beka's, and mine, are stitched together just like this quilt. Every square an event, a memory, a celebration.

"Beka will love it." Zack winks. "Nice work, both of you."

Although Katie did most of the work, I know Beka will appreciate my part in it. Katie taught me how to embroider a message on one of the white satin squares of fabric leftover from my wedding gown. I used watermelon color thread and embroidered the words, *We are moving toward the sunrise that will suddenly pierce our darkness and bless our souls with the glorious light of day.*

"Let's take it to her now," Katie says as she disappears into Beka's room.

"Why would Beka or I want kids when we have Katie? She'll always be our little darling." I smile at Sean.

Zack slaps Sean on the back. "I was thinking the same thing."

"Shelli. Sean. Zack." Katie shouts as she bolts from Beka's room. "You've gotta see this." She grabs my hand pulling me behind her.

"What?" I ask.

Katie leads us to the foot of the bed. "Beka was asleep when I came in, so Barry and I carefully removed the blanket from her bed and spread the quilt over her so she'd be surprised when she woke up. Only she surprised us. Come over here." Katie is practically jumping at the foot of Beka's bed. "Look!"

I see a twinkle in Beka's dark eyes. There's a soft smile on her face as Katie lifts the edge of the quilt.

When I look down, Beka wiggles her toes.

"Oh my God. Oh my God. Thank you." I say, as Katie and I hug each other then Beka. In all this excitement, I realize that I have thanked God out loud. Have I at last committed to my faith? Do I really believe that all this healing, all this happiness is God's faithfulness? Or did I speak words I've heard all my life that are ingrained in my mind?

"Look here," Barry says as he steps to the head of Beka's bed.

We watch as Beka's frail hand reaches out for us. "I love my slobber sisters."

When we squeeze her hand, she squeezes back.

# Epilogue

Today is the eve of another Yom Kippur. A year has passed since Beka first wiggled her toes and began her ascent out of darkness. Before my wedding, I thought that Beka, Katie, and I were bonded but nothing compares with the strength and unity that has settled into our lives this year. We still wonder about the faith of our fathers as set forth in the Torah and the Christian Bible and in the interpretation of both by organized religions. We have concluded that there is a universal creator with a plan beyond our frail comprehension—a supreme being who is good and kind and fair. One who silently roots for us as well as weeps for us. We know that no one is exempt from calamity. If we trudge on, holding to one another, we'll leave our winter socks behind and dance barefoot in the cool grass of spring.

The synapses of my mangled mind and the neurons of Beka's shattered spine realigned over the past year as we slobber sisters rediscovered a world of laughter. We still slobber sometimes but through our tears, we look for that proverbial rainbow. We know that everything does happen for a reason. Even adversity. We've learned that if we stand far enough back from any circumstance we will discover a new purpose and a deeper meaning to our lives.

We haven't forgotten the illness, the accident, or the pain we suffered but rather put them in their places in the ongoing saga of our lives. Each day we come closer to the realization that we were not forsaken. This is not to say that some supreme *good* shed light into our darkness to heal us but rather stood steadfast holding a lantern, hoping we would choose the light. In our enlightenment, we've set off into our next momentous adventures.

A few weeks after Beka's discharge from the hospital, she and I joined Katie for lunch at her place in Apex. We had worked all morning turning the all-white, spare bedroom into an ethereal aquarium of angelfish—an aqua nursery for the soon-to-arrive Laura-Kate.

Katie was nesting and had prepared a luncheon even Rachael Ray would envy.

As we sat around the dining room table admiring the wedding china, silver, and crystal, as well as Katie's culinary expertise, Beka confided a secret she'd long been harboring. She'd felt tingling in her toes and fingers since the morning before Barry's visit. She'd fallen in love with him and didn't trust that his interest in her was anything more than sympathy. He'd confessed his love for her a hundred times over the phone both before and after her accident. But she hadn't been convinced.

She had to see him, had to hear him tell her in person that he loved her after he saw her lifeless body. She wanted him to see the nurses feed her, bathe her, and empty the urine from the bag hanging from the bed. If he could stand all that, she knew there had to be hope for some sort of future, even if she never moved again.

"Barry is one of a kind." Katie plopped a spoonful of yogurt into her homemade tomato soup. "That first day he saw you in the hospital, he stuck around. Most men would've taken one look at you and run."

"But Barry didn't. Oy vay, I'm lucky."

"It wasn't luck, it was fate." Katie put down her spoon.

"Fate." I think a moment. "You're right, Katie. If it wasn't for Zack choosing Barry to help officiate at our wedding how would they have ever met?"

"That's only partially true." Beka looks to me. "Barry might not be in my life right now had it not been for my accident."

I dropped my fork when I heard the word accident.

"I'm really glad I gave him the chance to see me paralyzed." Beka reached for more cheese-filled bread, another of Katie's specialties. "Otherwise, I'd always wonder if he wasn't waiting to see if I'd recover."

"You were pretty brave. I don't think I could've done what you did." Katie smiles.

"Those first couple of days were difficult. I've never told you this but we did a lot of crying—first in despair then in hopefulness."

"You were already in love before the accident, weren't you?" I asked.

"Yeah, I just didn't want to believe it. I couldn't figure how it could work. I'd refused his romantic advances."

"So, the accident paved the way," Katie says. "Something good came from it."

Hearing these words, I grabbed my napkin to blow my nose."

"Don't you have any manners?" Beka sat tall with her hands on her hips. "That's so rude to blow your nose into a napkin, especially a brand-new linen one."

"Then you'd better get your tush up out of that chair and get me a tissue." I commanded with a big smile.

"Alright, I will." She did just that but watching her just made me slobber all the more. It was still difficult for me to believe that Beka could walk again.

Once back in her seat, she handed me a box of tissues. "It's really over, Shell."

"What a precious gift you gave us to start the New Year." I choke up, pull another tissue from the box.

The day Beka was discharged from the hospital, Barry picked her up in his arms and carried her out the front door. On their way to the car Beka called her mother to set into motion the surprise of our lives.

I answered my phone on the way home from class. Mrs. Schultzberg insisted that I drop everything, call Katie, Sean, Zack, and my parents, and meet her at the Morehead Manor B&B in Raleigh at six sharp. No excuses.

Instead of going home from the hospital that afternoon, Barry had hijacked a Rabbi who had befriended them both in the hospital. They drove to the Wake County Court House in Raleigh where they obtained a marriage license then reserved a room at the elegant B&B down the street.

When everyone arrived at the inn, we were led through antique-filled rooms to a large veranda that spanned the back of the building. Fifteen minutes later Beka and Barry were married under the quilt-turned-chuppah that Katie and I had made.

"When I'm strong enough to design and make our gowns, we'll have a proper wedding. But, for now," Beka said, "this is what we want to do."

Barry had left his city planning job and his congregation in Miami a month after visiting Beka in the hospital. He stayed with Zack and me until he found a job in Raleigh. He spent every spare moment with Beka. I honestly feel that her rehab moved along more swiftly because of Barry's positive vibes as well as the sense of humor they both possess.

It's been a long road but Beka can walk without help today. She's busy planning an extravagant wedding as well as starting her own company of fashion consultation with a specialty in bridal apparel. Already there are clients lined up at her door due to her online portfolio that just contains gowns from Katie's wedding and mine along with a few new sketches. Who knows, she may slip into haute couture through the back door.

A month later Katie called with good and humorous news. Her water broke while she was in the frozen food section of the new Super Target in Cary.

"I'm so embarrassed I don't know what to do."

"Listen to me." I tried to speak without laughing. "Just walk away like nothing happened."

"You mean just leave the cart here? It's full."

"Forget the cart. Walk slowly to your car. Are you in pain?"

"No, just mental pain. It's a good thing I have on black pants because they're soaked."

"Grab some plastic bags on your way out, to protect the car seat. Let me know when you're in the car." I bit my tongue to keep from laughing. I could imagine how embarrassed she was.

"I'm getting into my car."

"Great. Now call the mid-wife, see what you should do. Did you call Sean?"

"I had to leave a message. He's in a meeting."

"Call me back as soon as you can. I'll see if I can get to Sean through the switchboard, okay?"

When Katie hung up I made a quick call to Beka, asked her to stand by then left a message at Sean's office. It seemed like hours but was probably just five minutes before Katie called back.

"I have low back pain with a little cramping so the midwife wants to check me out at the hospital. Sean called. He's going to meet me there."

"Are you sure you can drive?"

"Yeah. I'm fine now. The hospital is just down the road."

"Do you want Beka and me to meet you there or is it too early?"

"I don't know. I don't want you to miss this big event."

"Done. I've already talked with Beka. She's standing by. We'll see you in a few minutes."

Just because Katie's water broke didn't mean that our Laura-Kate would be born imminently. We all rushed to Katie's bedside but it was eleven hours before Katie reached the pushing stage. Then she pushed for another hour. Zack and Barry paced in the waiting room, too queasy to realize that Katie's miracle wouldn't arrive in painless silence. By the thirteenth hour, Katie held her breath and pushed until her face turned purple. Next thing we knew, Laura-Kate was on Katie's chest while Sean's shaky hand cut the umbilical cord. The midwife caught the placenta in a metal basin while the labor nurse massaged Katie's fundus.

Laura-Kate had been set free. For a fleeting moment, while everyone else shed tears of joy, I saw this child alone, cut off from her life source, screaming from fear of being abandoned. For a moment I identified with her. I tried hard to put that thought out of my mind. I knew that a long line of loving hearts surrounded our little Laura-Kate.

Motherhood didn't stop with Katie. So much for my plan to start a family after my residency and so much for *safe* sex. By the time I graduated from medical school in my eighth month, I outweighed just about everyone in my class, even the guys.

For a graduation gift to myself, I arranged the celebration mikvah that I'd envisioned just after Beka's accident. With the graduation festivities over and three weeks before my baby was due, this seemed the ideal time for my vision to become reality. Beka, Katie, and I thought about our ritual for days. When we got it right, we wrote it down and memorized it but we couldn't bring ourselves to call it a mikvah. It was a celebration of healing—not an orthodox purification ceremony.

For our tent, we bought bolts of white gauze to drape over an umbrella-style tent frame and enough more to wrap around our bodies like togas. Beka made glorious headpieces out of twisted tulle and satin flowers while Katie and I shopped for fairy lights, white paper sacks for luminaries, candles, and six tall torches.

On the afternoon of our celebration, as we gathered our supplies, the sun behind my parent's condo burst into a gigantic orange fire that danced across the lavender and gold horizon, igniting our passion to begin our celebration. We set about filling the fifty or so white paper sacks half-full with sand and placed candles in each one then set our luminaries around our little tent. Our husbands strung the tiny white lights over the flowing white gauze tent. When all the candles were lit Zack plugged in the fairy lights. It was at that very moment, standing together in the center of the spectacle we'd created, that Beka, Katie, and I truly believed that we had been remembered. We had so much to celebrate, so much to be thankful for—we'd been overcome by darkness but we were not consumed by it. Our glowing faces were proof that we had broken free and stood in the light. Swathed in tulle, with our flowered wreaths, we held hands to say our ritual as we slowly walked into the blue water with the deep lavender and tangerine streaked sky sheltering us. As hard as we tried to make this a sacred, meaningful event, we giggled until we were splashing each other the way we'd done when we were ten. When our ritual was said and done we floated on our backs, held hands, lifted our right legs into the air then our left ones like an Olympic synchronized swim team.

Without forewarning, pain seized my pelvis. "Ouch."

"What?" Beka and Katie asked together.

"Too much garlic, I think," I said before feeling a gripping pain that tore through me like nothing I could have ever imagined causing me to double over in the shoulder-deep water. "Ouch. Hold me up."

Beka grabbed my arm while Katie put a hand to my huge belly as another pain flashed through me.

"You're having contractions, Shelli." Katie puckered her brow. "Let's get you out of the water."

The pain eased up for a moment, just long enough for me to walk to our glowing tent. The tulle that once draped me like a dress hung from my neck as Katie spread out a beach towel for me to lie on. Katie worriedly placed both her hands on my now rigid belly as another contraction ripped and my water broke.

"I think you're going to have this baby right now," Katie said as she placed a dry towel against my bottom. "You're crowning."

"We need to call 911," Beka shouted to our husbands on the deck.

Zack came running, his face pale, horror-struck.

"Everything's under control," I said as calmly as I felt. I don't remember being happier. I was having my baby in this glowing candlelight with my two best friends beside me, their faces aglow, togas soaking wet and decorated with seaweed, wreathes haphazard on their beautiful heads. My heart tried to leap right out of my body. Another contraction started at my breastbone. I felt it in slow motion as it rippled the muscles of my abdomen and burned my pelvis in agonizing fulfillment. I didn't scream out but bore the pain in a strange, expectant way.

I looked to Zack, who had stopped in the doorway, eyes glazed. "Come sit by me. Hold my hand." He did just that as another contraction then another ripped and burned. I held my breath and pushed the way I'd seen Katie push.

As the contractions became stronger, threatening to rip me to shreds, I smiled with teeth gritted.

We heard Laura-Kate crying. The sound of it caused Katie to clench her breast. "Bring her to me," Katie shouted, obviously afraid to leave my side. "And bring a string or a shoelace to tie the cord. This baby is coming right now."

Sean arrived with the squalling Laura-Kate. Barry was right behind him with a shoelace.

"We're having another baby." I smiled. "You guys can come in if you want." I wanted to share this precious event with the whole wide world.

"No, thanks," Sean said nervously. "I'll be on the deck boiling the water. Barry is going to flag down the paramedics."

"Come on, Bek," Katie instructed, holding Laura-Kate to her breast. "You watched Laura come out. You have to help with this one."

Beka froze. "I don't know if I can do what the midwife did."

"All you have to do is catch," I instructed. "I'll push her out. I can do this. So can you." Before the next contraction, I looked about the tent to see faces I didn't recognize—young faces of my ancestors, here to comfort me and to celebrate.

"This is it. I have to push." Excruciating pain ripped and tugged on my racing heart. I closed my eyes and pushed with all my might until everything went black. From the recesses of my mind came Sarah, Hagar, Esther and Elizabeth, Mama and Saphira, then a familiar voice—Naomi's. I felt as if I was floating out beyond the breakers in the calm, protective, turquoise sea. I watched as my beautifulists Naomi spread the sparkling, translucent drape over the top of the tent as peacefulness surround me.

"Shelli, Shelli." Katie frantically patted my face. "Wake up. Stay with us. Push. Come on. One more big push."

I drew in as much air as possible and pushed through the most excruciating, awesome pain imaginable as my baby passed from me. When I opened my eyes Zack had our baby girl in his hands, his eyes glossy. "She's here." He laid her on my chest. Katie dried her with a beach towel.

"I love you, Shelli. Thank you for this gift." Zack held my face in his hands and kissed me a hundred times.

Again, I was plagued with the thought that, just like Laura-Kate, my daughter's cry was from the cutting off of her life source and the fear of abandonment. I shook my head to clear it. I smiled when I realized the reality of the moment—if darkness shall one day fall upon her, Zack and I will hold her up. If that's not enough, Katie and Beka, Mama, Saphira, and Rachael will too. That fleeting fear was the last of my irrational thinking.

My sickness began with the death of my beautifulists niece, Naomi, and ended with the blessed birth of her cousin. I rose up on one elbow. Zack knelt behind me so I could lean against him. This mysterious precipitous birth seemed to heal my mind completely and seal my wholeness.

Zack touched me in a way that said he understood the healing that had taken hold of me. I felt overwhelmed by my beautifulists Naomi's revelation of herself from beyond the boundaries of this life and this earth. She stood, like Beka, Katie, and me, remembered by generations of women before her and generations of women who will come after her. As I gazed into my baby's sweet face I reveled in joy that she too was known to them and would be remembered by them. "Shall we name her Sarah?" I asked Zack and he nodded.

Our beautiful Sarah nuzzled her way to my breast. When she latched on, my uterus cramped in gladness.

"You're next, you know." I looked to Beka.

She wiped her eyes with the back of her hand. "I know—just as soon as I'm strong enough."

Tears streamed my face. There we were—the three of us, sitting together, fulfilling our legacies. When times are positive it's easy to believe in a universe of love. I knew then that when darkness comes to us again, we'll be ready for the worst of it, that we'll know to hold fast, to see the love of our creator in each other's reaching out. This seemed the beginning of our celebration. Our darkness past. Our futures bright with hope. I smiled up at my beautifulists Naomi, knowing that she would entertain Beka's daughter until the time was right for her deliverance into the world of the second generation of slobber sisters.

With Sarah at my breast and Zack supporting me and loving me, I reeled in wellness. I knew that I was worthy of this magnificent gift of contentment. I began the ritual again. Katie and Beka joined in. This time we didn't giggle. This time we were reverent.

"Together we stand to take our places before the great lineage of strong women who have come before us. As we enter these healing waters we ask to be cleansed of vanity and faithlessness. Our souls long, yea, faint for the courts of our mothers and sisters on earth and beyond. Our hearts sing in joyful thanksgiving of their attendance to us in our days of darkness and in our triumphant battle.

There were three friends, parted by insanity and folly.
One doomed to die from transmutation.
One doomed to die from injury.
One doomed to die from a broken heart.
Yet each reached out to the others and said,
'Let me die in your stead.'

The universe was deeply moved.
The creator said, 'You have healed each other and made
yourselves whole. Now is the time to laugh. For only
those who have hands to hold will be able to laugh'.

And we laughed.

Thank you for reading Transmutare. If you have enjoyed this novel both the author and the publisher would appreciate a review on Amazon.com.

## About the Author

Shelia Bolt Rudesill is an accidental writer. For forty-five years as a pediatric and NICU nurse, she dedicated her professional life to the wellbeing of children and acquired a tremendous empathy for those burdened with unreasonable hardships. Her writing career began at the age of fifty when her cousin, Dottie, encouraged her to chronicle the poignant experiences she encountered in her professional and social life. "Just about everyone I know," Shelia says, "provides a situation or trait for a character in one of my novels."
In addition to reading and writing, Shelia admits to a weakness for dry martinis, evening gowns, and dancing with cats.

Other novels by Shelia:

Baggage
Child of My Heart
Auspicious Dreams
All The Voices In My Head

www.ingramcontent.com/pod-product-compliance
Lightning Source LLC
Chambersburg PA
CBHW070817180626
46818CB00001B/305